RAD DAD

RAD DAD

Dispatches from the
Frontiers of Fatherhood

Edited by Tomas Moniz and Jeremy Adam Smith

PM Press
Microcosm Publishing
2011

For my son, Liko, who gave me a new life.
  —Jeremy

I dedicate this book to Dylan, Zora, and Ella for keeping me true and heckling me when I wasn't.
  —Tomas

Rad Dad: Dispatches from the Frontiers of Fatherhood
© 2011 Jeremy Adam Smith and Tomas Moniz
This edition © 2011 PM Press

ISBN: 978-1-60486-481-6
LCCN: 2011927948

Cover art by Nikki McClure
Cover and interior design by Josh MacPhee/Justseeds.org

PM Press
PO Box 23912, Oakland, CA 94623
www.pmpress.org

Microcosm Publishing
636 SE 11th Ave., Portland, OR 97214-2405
www.microcosmpublishing.com

Printed on recycled paper by the Employee Owners of Thomson-Shore in Dexter, Michigan.
www.thomsonshore.com

10 9 8 7 6 5 4 3 2

Contents

Tweens and Teens

Politics of Parenting: Gender, Race, Allies, Visions

Interviews with Rad Dads

INTRODUCTION

The Politics of *Rad Dad*, or Parenting Is about More than Pee, Poop, and Puberty
Tomas Moniz

The book you hold in your hands combines the best pieces from my zine *Rad Dad*, which I started five years ago, with some additional contributions from the blog *Daddy Dialectic*, which Jeremy started four years ago—two kindred publications that have tried to explore parenting as political territory. Both of these projects have pushed the conversation around fathering beyond the safe, apolitical focus most books and websites stick to. Both have worked hard to create a diverse, multifaceted space in which to grapple with the complexity of fathering.

Of course, not everything is serious. I have sold lots of zines with stories of my son battling a bout of explosive bowel moments in Chiapas or my daughter wanting her first bra or my youngest daughter asking awkward questions within earshot of the subject of those questions, like, *why do some boys wear eyeliner?* And the truth is I like writing (and reading) about those things. They're funny, people get a kick out of them, and I usually seem smarter than I actually am—but those very same situations or questions usually also allude to larger political issues that are a little more difficult to address. With *Rad Dad*, I've always wanted to move beyond sharing stories about bodily functions—as pleasurable as they might be—and into the realm of how our parental choices embody or contradict or challenge our values and political intentions.

I understand why many parents might resist putting politics and parenting together. Sometimes it feels overwhelming to just make my kids dinner, let alone consider the implications of taking them to their favorite fast food joint. Sometimes I regret the choices I've made; sometimes I regret them even while I'm making them. My parenting has always been rife with contradictions, like debating whether to put our six-month-old in daycare five days a week so we both could stay in school, or whether to rent *Mean Girls* for the tenth time (because Lindsay Lohan is such a good role model for preteen girls!). It seems like I make choices every day that challenge what I believe and how I aspire to parent. However, I'd like to think that parenting is a lot like revising an essay: you gotta come back to things again and again. You rephrase, rethink, at times regret, but you're always willing to return and reconsider.

I'll be honest, it has been terrifying at times to examine the political implications embodied in my relationship with my children, their mother, and notions of family in general. Those are the moments when I want to tell stories about pee and poop and puberty, just to avoid the scary stuff. In the first issue of *Rad Dad*, I confessed that I waited years for someone else to do a zine that would foster parents', and particularly fathers', political awareness. I'll tell you why I was so hesitant: I wasn't sure how to talk about parenting without it sounding narcissistic or self-satisfied or privileged—*See, look, I change diapers, aren't I a good father?* or *Let me tell you about how I once got up and rocked the baby to sleep*—while the mother still did the majority of housecleaning, errands, and other parental responsibilities.

I knew I wasn't alone in this fear. Many fathers I met were uncomfortable writing about parenting because of this issue—as well as the internalized belief that we fathers don't have much to offer or say about parenting. In the first post to his blog *Daddy Dialectic*, my coeditor Jeremy said something similar: "Friends had suggested that I should write about being a mostly stay-at-home dad. Until last week, I always said, *No, I'm not going to write about being a dad; not yet, anyway* . . . Even in liberal, genderfucking San Francisco, I'm still usually the only dad in Liko's music and swim classes, and usually the only one at the playground before 5 p.m. . . . As a stay-at-home dad, I'm supposed to be a trend [but] it's a pretty small fucking trend."

So for us, *Rad Dad* and *Daddy Dialectic*—like Ariel Gore's pioneering zine *Hip Mama*—are not just about parenthood. They're also about fighting the social power that men have over women—and beyond *that*, challenging all of the ways that some people have power over others. This book is a forum for men to reconsider intimately what it means to be successful and how capitalist notions of success are tied to the construction of male identity. It's a place to question the social stereotypes of fathering that for so long have been used to justify gender-specific parental roles.

For example, there is nothing inherently wrong with a man providing the main income for a family and a woman being the primary caretaker. But this book says the decision needs to be transparent, needs to be a choice and not the default. Fathers need to actively consider what might be the underlying reasons for their decisions, about their priorities and how they father. But more than that, this book tries to help dads see the ways in which our fathering is inextricably tied to issues of social and environmental justice. The bestselling *What to Expect When You're Expecting* lists every possible illness and injury that can kill or cripple your child—but it doesn't address the fact that children of color grow up with fewer services, poorer schools, more toxicity, more street violence and, as they grow older, fewer job opportunities than their white counterparts. Basically, I want people to step back when we announce we're fathers and that we're here and we ain't leaving until some things change. These are lofty goals, but what better place to start than with ourselves?

So here it is. Read it to your kids (I did), your friends, give it to the men in your life as well as the women; forget gender and just give it to everybody. We give you this book as a prototype, hoping that it will lead to that community I still long to be a part of, circles where we fathers can chew on parenting that isn't based in sexist, outdated gender biases, and yet that can be honest and open about those same pressures and images we face daily. I hope this continues with me and other fathers, because I know there are so many rad dads trying to parent in these dangerous times in loving, meaningful, authentic, and ultimately revolutionary ways.

Section One

BIRTH, BABIES, AND TODDLERS

Notes from a Sperm Donor
Keith Hennessy

Several times in the past twenty years I've been asked by straight and queer women to provide sperm for their baby-making. Until I was forty, I said no. Figuring out what family is or can be has always been problematic for me, a dissident gay male artist actively resisting masculine expectations while still prioritizing an art career. Donating sperm seemed too emotionally complicated and wrapped in my own desire for kids. Then one day a close friend, whom I'll call S., asked me to help her and her partner to have a baby. I surprised myself by saying yes.

And then we did it. Which means I came into a bowl, and then one woman, using a small syringe (I don't think anyone uses turkey basters), shot my cum inside her lover. Then we held hands, wished for a baby, and I left them to orgasm on their own. Conception happened the first time we tried. I'm not sure which day. I mean it happened on one of the four days that we did it. It's not always that easy. We—my boymanfriend and I—later tried to help another dyke couple that had already spent too much money and time on frozen sperm. They also got pregnant on the first round but miscarried within weeks. Subsequent attempts, although fun and bonding between our two creative queer couples, didn't result in a child.

There were days when my partner would ask, why aren't *we* having a baby? It was a question we never resolved. Maybe because I was already in my mid-forties, and he had recently survived cancer, and our incomes from freelance artist and teaching gigs didn't amount to much. Maybe it was because the seeds of our breakup had already been planted and we didn't have a strong enough commitment to support a child. During that time I also continued to explore the idea of being a queer uncle. I would watch the ways that my manfriend and I engaged kids and youth in our art projects and the ways that we interacted with our various nieces and nephews. I recognized a need for adults who are not parents to queer the space between adults and children and social institutions. I like being a role model for nonnormative affection and desire.

I think I only saw S. once while she was pregnant. The moms live in Los Angeles and I live in San Francisco, so I wasn't involved in their day-to-day lives. I told a few close friends but I didn't talk much about it, or even think that much about it, until the birth. After the baby was born, everyone wanted to know if I'd seen him and o my god how was it? Was it OK? Did he look like you? Some friends had been so concerned about me. I told them, yes, I saw him and he was asleep in the baby wrap and S. looked so normal as a mom and it was just so normal for me to hold her baby. And then he squirmed a little and he got a diaper change so I got to see him all naked and fresh. And yes somewhere there was this quiet shyness and awkwardness and somewhere deep inside I was aware of something happening, emotional and magical, but I felt protected and blessed.

I also felt protective of the moms. When I say protective I'm referring to the subtle yet relentless violence of the questions we were asked. People incessantly asked the moms, "Who's the father?" while I was being asked, "What's it like to be a father?" And this word *father* was filled with ill-considered assumptions and opinions. It was hard not to be defensive. I'm not a father, I wanted to say, I'm a sperm donor. He's not my child. I don't know who he looks like. He has her coloring. And actually he has traits that seem more like the mom's partner. Although California has many laws and practices that support nonhetero parenting, the history of prioritizing biology over family, intention, and love is thick with hate. It's surprising how many of us "alternative" folk can casually use language that erases queer desire and family, and that reinforces very specific ideas of what is a mother and a father. And by those standards, I am not a father, not a dad. Just a guy who jerked off for his friends as part of a larger strategy of feminist and dyke solidarity.

When they heard the news, my family seemed mostly thrilled yet also confused. My sisters seemed to get it more, because they're more worldly and queer-conscious, and because they're both feminists and mothers. One sister asked if it was appropriate to send her own congratulations card. My brother's wife, who also just had a son, wanted to know if in fact the boys are cousins, and if so, can they have a play date someday, somewhere? Good questions. There's no consensus on the ethics and etiquette of DIY baby- and family-making outside the married hetero norms. In the midst of all this, my family continues to smile. Everyone loves babies, and my family loves family-making. I've always been queering family, so even though this chapter is new, there's nothing but well wishing and positive curiosity.

Sometimes I'm concerned that people, including my siblings, think that *I* have a baby. Many people congratulate me—which is a form of blessing, for sure, but it's also weird. I mean, for what? I was introduced to someone recently and she said, "Oh, you're Keith. Well, congratulations." Not thinking about the new baby, I looked very puzzled and said, "Thanks, what for?" Then she got embarrassed and said, "I must be confused." Only later did I realize that she knows the baby's parents and it probably seemed like I just didn't want to talk about it in front of the others we were with.

I see it as a big delightful improvisation, with so much unknowing, but that doesn't help to explain. To folks who act like I'm now a parent, I tell them that I gave my sperm up for adoption, or I tell them that I simply helped my good friends have a baby, or I tell them that the child has two parents, that I'm neither of them. The boy is now five years old. He's happy and creative and imaginative. It's a delight to see him and play a couple times a year. I keep a current photo on my wall or fridge just like I do with the kids of other friends, but I know that somewhere I hold a slightly more precious place for him. I don't use the words biodad or even uncle because they either confuse or mislead, and continue to confer an importance to biology that our trans friends have reminded us to let go of.

I'm reminded of one of my teachers, the pioneering aerial dancer Terry Sendgraff. She once told me that her students were her children. I love Terry for being an inspiring and supportive queer aunt. Her witness and encouragement of my work is motherly, in the best sense. In recent years I've put a lot of energy into mentoring young artists, and I often joke that I have children in all the countries where I travel to teach. I have a magnetic daddy vibe, whether it's a two-year-old who wants to play, a twenty-seven-year-old who seeks mentorship, or a thirty-seven-year-old woman whose baby clock is ticking.

But where do we get the desire to be a father? To plant our seed and reproduce from our own genetics and family lineage? I watch some of my straight guy friends wrestle with this and I'm surprised that I feel a little wave of contentment that I actually did it. That I reproduced. Regardless of how queer the situation. And I think this is something that others feel too, including my siblings, although no one actually speaks it. Being a sperm donor continues to provoke self-reflection and social reflection that I value.

Born in the Caul: My Journey Inside
Jason Denzin

I used to think of birth as something women and doctors did. Like the new fathers in the movies, I subconsciously believed that men simply waited outside or watched. As I became more aware of issues surrounding birth and pregnancy, I learned that men play a much more important role in the pregnancy and birth process than I'd previously thought. But, that new role was still a relatively outside role . . . helping to decide stuff like whether or not we go through with the pregnancy, which midwife to choose and the countless other baby-related choices that need to be made. When Genelle told me she was pregnant, I suddenly felt inspired, full of energy, happy, scared, and awed. I never imagined I would feel this way! I noticed that these feelings were coming from inside, not outside of me. And once I'd experienced this surprisingly transformative power of pregnancy and birth over myself as a man and a father-to-be, I didn't want to go back.

We found ourselves a home-birth midwife and enrolled in the closest thing to an alternative parenting class we could find. In the months leading up to the birth, I discovered how strong Genelle is and how capable her body is of going through the changes that are necessary for pregnancy and birth. Oh, and I found out that I really enjoyed making love to my newly pregnant partner. I had heard stories about men not wanting to have sex with their pregnant partners or pregnant women not wanting sex. But for us, it seemed to work out just right and the sex was wonderful.

I also began thinking of myself as a father and of how I might interact with my child. Genelle's son, Nick, was eight years old at the time, and I was beginning to get used to the idea of being a parent. For the past two years, I'd been involved in Nick's life, whether it was helping him with his homework or playing with him with his toys. We had a lot of fun together. I was slowly learning that being a parent didn't have to be a dreaded position of authority with life or death responsibility and no fun. Nick helped me learn that it's best for me to be myself, mistakes and all, so that both he and I could learn from them. He was very helpful in turning my perception of my parents as these perfect, untouchable, authoritarian people on its head.

One hot Sunday afternoon, 115 degrees in the sun—about two weeks before the ultrasound due date and four weeks prior to our midwife-predicted due date—we decided it would be a great idea to take a small road trip into the desert. Our midwife was on vacation, but I figured we had plenty of time until the baby was born.

Genelle had been feeling a bit uncomfortable in the car and when we got home, she told me she thought she might be experiencing false labor pains. Even though she was on vacation, our midwife took our call. She agreed with Genelle about the false labor discomfort because we were still two to four weeks away from the due date. She told us to start timing the surges and to let her know if they were coming closer together.

We started timing. Even though Genelle seemed to be uncomfortable, she handled it well and I agreed that it was probably a false labor. I helped Nick get ready for bed and started watching something on TV. I don't remember why I was watching TV except that I found that it helped me to relieve some of the stress from work and this new family life I was experiencing. And also, I guess, because it was there.

We called our midwife a few more times and each time she held onto the belief that this was false labor. Even though she wasn't in the room to make a really good judgment, we trusted her experience and her knowledge. After a few more time-recordings, and with no end in sight to Genelle's discomfort, our midwife told us to go ahead and call the backup midwife to come over just in case. To Genelle's surprise, the backup midwife insisted that we keep timing and call her back when we got more accurate times.

At the backup midwife's suggestion, Genelle got into the bath in an effort to relax, but it didn't seem to work; she remained uncomfortable and worried about the midwife not being there. I sat next to the tub, trying to offer any comfort I could, and Nick was sleeping in his bedroom. I was beset by uncontrollable, misplaced frustrations, a little bit peeved at Genelle for not being able to distinguish an actual from a false labor. While I was inside myself wishing everything was going smoothly and that she would magically regain control over her body, she made a loud moan and told me that she felt the baby moving down as mucous (or something) came out of her.

I called the backup midwife and told her that she better come over *now*—though we didn't even know how far away she lived from us and she had never been to our house before.

I rushed out of the bathroom and gently woke up Nick. I told him as calmly as I could that we were having the baby tonight and I needed him to come out of his room in order to answer the front door when the backup midwife arrived. He was happy to help and later told us that he had been awake for a while and was wondering what was happening. Once I got him situated at the front door and explained to him what to do, I returned to the bathroom.

At this point, I started to feel very, very nervous. Genelle was in the tub and thought the baby might be coming really soon. I realized at that moment that the baby might come out before the midwife got there and that we would have to trust in the universe and Genelle's body that all will be as it will be and we will deal with whatever it is. I mumbled something to this effect to Genelle, who probably didn't hear me at this point because she was now focusing on strong surges. After one of them, I looked and I saw something that looked like the very tip of a head.

"OK," I thought. "That's the baby."

But it didn't look like a baby. I had seen plenty of birth videos before from our midwife and in the birthing classes and I didn't remember babies looking like that! I thought, "Oh no, something must be wrong." I didn't say this because I knew how important it was to be calm and help Genelle be as comfortable as possible. But I considered all of the horrible things that could be wrong and how messed up the baby might be. As soon as those thoughts entered my mind, I pushed them out and forced myself to focus on Genelle and the baby. "Everything was going to be as it should be, this is a natural process, everyone will end up the way they will end up . . . relax . . . relax," I thought. I called the backup midwife and let her know that we could now feel the head. She said she was on her way. What else could she say? In fact, we were on our own.

Almost as soon as I hung up, Genelle experienced another big surge. Now, I could see a round ball that looked like a head, but not quite. It had this purplish-bluish thin sack around it. I had never seen anything like this in the videos. As I gently touched the sack, I realized that I could see hair through the sack. That was my baby's hair!

"This is really amazing!" I told Genelle, "I can see the baby's hair!"

Genelle was between surges so I just enjoyed the moment, awkward as it seemed, and realized that because I'd never seen something like this before, this may be the last time I see either of them alive. I will never forget that moment, the very first time I saw Paxten, alone with Genelle in the bathtub, amidst the swirling emotions of fear, excitement, Genelle's discomfort and fear of not having the midwife there, and my complete connection to Genelle and Paxten.

Again, I called the backup midwife and this time she remained on speakerphone and told me to tell Genelle to go ahead and push.

I told the midwife that the head was still inside a sack and the midwife assured me that it was OK. Genelle pushed during the next surge and Paxten moved out a little further. The midwife told me to try and break the sack. As I felt around the emerging baby, I must have gently hit something because all of the sudden, the sack popped and now I could see the baby just like in the videos.

Paxten was face down and I could see the cord wrapped around the back of his neck. I gently removed the cord because I could see that it might be preventing him from coming out, and out he popped, right into my hands.

At this point, I was in some kind of strange trance-like-calm-everything's-fine mode. In the homebirth videos I saw, the midwife places the baby on the mother's chest. So I immediately did this and Genelle was so very happy and relieved. So was I. And apparently, so was Paxten, who coughed a little, gave a little cry, and then started breathing normally. His skin started turning what I thought was a really healthy color. All seemed to be well for now.

The backup midwife was still on the phone and told me to put a blanket over Paxten. I rushed around the house looking for a blanket. While searching, I passed the front door, where Nick was patiently waiting, and told him that Paxten had been born.

He said, "Is it a boy or a girl?" Genelle and I hadn't even checked. We were so happy to see Paxten that we didn't even care at that point. But since Nick asked, I walked back into the bathroom with the blanket I'd found, took a quick peek and saw that it was a boy. I also noticed that the bathtub seemed to be kind of bloody and dirty, so I told Nick to continue waiting for the midwife by the front door and to stay out of the bathroom. Genelle seemed to be just fine, she was much more comfortable at this point and did not indicate any signs of suffering. Now, we only had to wait for the midwife to get there.

Almost two years later, we had another child at home, a wonderful girl named Raen. All of us are as healthy as can be. I'm grateful that Genelle spared me the potentially humiliating, disempowering, and dangerous experience of birth in a hospital. While writing this, I could feel the chills from the experience as if I was watching from over my shoulder and it was happening right now. When I look at Paxten, I still see his beautiful hair as I gently pushed down on the sack. I now look at coworkers, strangers, and friends and wonder about their birth experiences both as babies and as parents. This vision helps me to remember how connected every being really is. We found out later that a small percentage of babies are born with the amniotic sack still in place—or, as it is called, "born in the caul."

I'm glad I didn't follow the vision of myself waiting outside during birth. I took a leap into the unknown and now know that everything is as it is. I'm deeply aware of and humbled by the power of pregnancy and birth to transform all involved, including men. And on top of that, I discovered that we can go inside any experience together in order to handle what comes to us as a team and, more importantly, as a family.

Everyday Revolution
Mark Andersen

When you become a father, your life starts over. You see yourself as a child in your child and you see your parents in yourself. As a one-time teenage punk who fiercely rebelled against my parents and their rural, working-class pieties of family, duty, and self-sacrifice, I now find myself increasingly inspired by their example. This odd turnabout, however, only scratches the surface of a revolution that is a daily journey into radical humility and deeper understanding.

This upheaval was sparked by the arrival of an "outside agitator": my son, Soren Huseyin Luis Ozdeger-Andersen, adopted as a newborn fourteen months ago. His cumbersome name suggests much history and expectation: Soren, in honor of my father, son of Danish immigrants, also recalling the philosopher Kierkegaard; Huseyin for my wife Tulin's Turkish father; and Luis, the name his Mexican-American birth mother chose for him. This serious mouthful is crowned by a six-syllable hyphenated last name: Ozdeger-Andersen. All of this disparate history is embodied in a baby-now-turning-into-little-boy.

Our journey to Soren and parenthood was long and hard. Although I was in my mid-forties when we began to try to get pregnant, Tulin is more than a decade younger. Being in good health and with no obvious issues, we assumed our new quest would be fun and relatively easy.

It was not to be, however. Several years later—after stumbling through a maze of timed intercourse, numerous medical consults, stressful fertility treatments, naturopathic remedies, and more, we had to surrender our original dream. It had been expensive, heart-wrenching, and ultimately unsuccessful in anything other than enriching our credit card companies. Above all, it was deeply humbling, and a powerful jolt to us as a couple: we were not capable of getting pregnant, this seemingly simple thing, one which happened naturally and unplanned to so many, even when they sought to avoid it.

Marriages have often foundered on such shoals. Somehow, we made it through together, and after a period of grieving launched into a new challenge: the world of adoption. While this path was also certainly not without expense, and required massive paper-pushing, social-work assessments, and medical tests, it also held the hope of an actual child at the end of the road, one that desperately needed good parents.

But the process also opened new Pandora's boxes of uncertainty. Should we pursue international or domestic options? What did we think about cross-racial adoption? What agency should we work with, what degree of openness with birth parents, what flexibility to risk factors like drug use, more . . . and finally, inevitably, what are the political implications? The complicated choices made me dizzy, and deeply tested our connection as a couple once again.

One by one, our concerns were addressed and we made our choices. Soon we were working with two great agencies, the Barker Foundation in the D.C. area and A Act of Love in Utah, both of which put first priority on providing support for birth parents but also work sensitively and tirelessly with adoptive parents like us.

While, in principle, adoption results in that longed-for child, so much was, again, out of our control. First of all, birth parents—usually a mother, as few fathers seemed engaged—had to choose you, so months, perhaps years, of waiting were to be expected. Then, even after being chosen, even after the baby's birth, there was an excruciating period where the birth mother could change her mind, and sometimes did. If that happened, you would be left with nothing but an ache in your heart, and additional mountains of debt.

For us, of course, the story found a happy ending—and new beginning—on January 13, 2010, when Soren was born at a hospital in Maricopa County, Arizona. The extraordinary beauty of that day is burned into my heart and soul. Meeting this tiny new human and his birth mom on that day, sharing dreams and hopes, growing comfortable with one another, holding Soren for the first time, suckling him . . . then taking him home with us a few days later, struggling to help him sleep that first night, trying everything till he finally fell asleep on my legs, as I sat upright on a couch in our hotel room . . . the words and emotions come tumbling out in a rush, blurring into beautiful chaos, just like those first giddy days together.

The magic was real . . . but talk about a revolution! In the space of one day, even the simplest task now had to be totally rethought, to factor in this beautiful new piece of the puzzle, to make sure he was nourished, loved, and protected. No matter how many books I read, how many classes or support groups I attended, I couldn't ever have been prepared for that new reality. Fortunately, the immense love I immediately felt pulled me through those first sleepless nights, the doubting of myself as a competent parent, the ever-present fear of something horrific going wrong.

Tulin and I decided to rearrange our work schedules to be Soren's primary caretakers, sharing the role equally, with only twelve hours of paid help spread out over the week. Having gone through so much to become parents, we were eager to be there for his unfolding as a person, even though it meant serious self-sacrifice.

I, in particular, needed to be present for my son in ways that my own father was not. I say this without condemnation, for our family finances were then so slender that my dad's incessant labors were probably essential for our survival. Still, I missed him immeasurably, even though I often felt somehow not worthy, not good enough, in his presence. The one time I can recall Dad pausing from work to play basketball with my brother and me—albeit for less than a minute—is a treasured memory.

Equally precious is a conversation many years later—I was then well into my thirties—when Dad confided that he had wanted to be around more, but that his work, his bread-winning, was the main way he knew how to show his love for us. This was an astonishingly intimate admission for my dad. After all, we had never even hugged one another until I was twenty-one . . . and then only because I initiated it, after building up the courage to give the hug over the previous six months!

This proved to be something of a breakthrough moment, for my father slowly but surely became more physically and verbally demonstrative over the following years. As Dad grew able to express his love consistently and convincingly, we grew ever closer in the last years before his death from lung cancer in 2004. Still, I hope Soren never has the questions I had, but feels my love, experiences it daily, in word and in deed. Simply, I want to be there for him now and always.

Trying to balance my own very considerable workload with this desire is hardly easy, however, for either my wife or me. Although having no regrets about our decision, I've learned the hard way just how difficult and damaging to a marriage the arrival of a child can be, and thus to one's own spiritual/emotional balance . . . much less to any aspirations of contributing toward larger social transformation.

Moreover, just being in the same physical space with my son is not the same as being authentically present for him and the mystery and miracle of his growth. How can I uphold "the revolution" while sleep-deprived, struggling to keep on decent terms with my mate, trying to get work done, helping make sure there is money to pay the bills . . . all while being truly there for my son? I'm not exactly sure—but I accept the overriding imperative to provide Soren the love, respect, and security he needs and deserves every day, as a new person, learning as he goes along, dealing daily with the newest challenge.

There is humor to be savored in all of this, whenever I find the grace to do so. For example, I regularly expose my son to anthems of my would-be-revolution, including the Clash, Fugazi, Chumbawamba, Bikini Kill, and more. But if the first song Soren ever heard was "Destroy Babylon" by Bad Brains, other tunes now rule our house and my own subconscious. "Hello Everybody," "Pop Goes the Weasel," "Don Alfredo Baila," and countless other children's songs run through my brain at all hours, on an endless loop.

Nor can I just let these songs wash over me. No, if Soren is to be truly satisfied, often I must engage with them, sing along, act them out. Sometimes the only thing that can console him is a vigorously rendered "Old McDonald" lyrically adapted to proclaim, "Grandpa Merlin/Grandma Margaret had a farm," in honor of my father and mother. One especially turbulent and largely sleepless night I sang the song for Soren so long that my voice was worn down to a ragged whisper.

Of course, there is a genuine joy in this play, if I am open to it, willing to dive in and embrace the *now*. To nurture this kind of concentration, to see past the spectacular to relish the small wonders; this is no easy task. However, it is deeply transformative.

Interacting with my son teaches me that it is a work/play well worth taking on . . . and as at least as relevant to true revolution as mounting the barricades.

In his powerful book *Eating Animals*, Jonathan Safran Foer wrote that becoming a father made him "want to be better," deepening his commitment to animals and the environment, to living out that compassionate life more fully. I can relate, for every fiber of my being wants to build that new world that I have so long struggled for, talked about, and pushed toward, if only because I so deeply desire that to be the world that surrounds and embraces my precious son.

Yet, I find this emotion powerfully—if sometimes paradoxically—in tension with other imperatives. The reality is that while barricades sometimes still call—after all, this is written as courageous people across the Middle East and North Africa are rising up for freedom, risking their lives for the hope of a better future—my life is now fundamentally tied to that quest for transformation within one of the most typical and widely shared of human activities: parenthood. To be a father means to temper many of my own public aspirations, to step back a bit from the edge, to adjust my work as to do whatever is necessary to stand with and be there for Soren, to build a foundation for his possibilities.

This is profoundly humbling because I must do all of this while knowing in the end, I will never control—nor should I really try—my child's ultimate choices. I can give all my love, all my sleepless nights, all of the struggle to balance work and home in order to be able to love Soren more deeply and truly . . . and my son may turn out to reject everything I stand for, spitting on my dreams and visions.

And if this pains me to think of, even for a moment, then waiting just past that fear is an unwelcome ache of recognition. Suddenly, the suffering I caused my parents—by doing almost exactly what I pray my son won't do—socks me in the face. The taste in my mouth stings like blood, and the shock of collision resonates, carrying the inescapable flavor and feel of that most revolutionary of all commodities: truth.

Suddenly, I am no longer the righteous rebel, but the potential oppressor, the traitor who might betray the future entrusted to me in the form of this smart, strong, mischievous, stubborn yet extraordinarily vulnerable child. No longer am I so comfortable critiquing my parents; now I fear that, for all my big ideas and loudly proclaimed ideals, I may not do as good a job as they did under much more objectively difficult circumstances.

One fear cuts especially deeply, persisting to this day: my worries about raising a son in this world where male children so often are schooled in all manner of ugliness and stupidity—perhaps especially within gang-ridden inner-city communities such as where I now live—a condition which is often excused under the euphemism "masculinity." Decades before, I had rebelled against the often destructive macho construct of maleness in my rural home, driven by bitter experience of its lash. Despite all that has come to pass in the past three decades—such as a zine called *Rad Dad*, unthinkable when I was a teenage boy—male roles still are hardly the epitome of human possibility.

While I surely wish that Soren would not have to go through this, even more intimate worries lurk below my concern for him: essentially, could I be a good dad to my son, given that my ambivalence toward masculinity is so intense? After all, my isolation and rejection had run unhealthily deep, driven partly by an insecurity that I could never live up to my father's expectations; now I am supposed to raise a healthy, balanced son?

Moreover, as an older dad—now in my early fifties due to the long quest to reach parenthood—will I live long enough to truly be there for Soren, to see him grow into a man, a kind, sensitive, strong and compassionate male human, maybe someday birthing his own family, my grandchildren? The absence of my own father—who died several years before Soren's arrival, but thankfully not before we had fully reconciled—still aches, decades into my adult years.

My father's "work will set you free" ethic and my mother's religion-based sense of duty, their insistence on sacrificing self in order to look out for others—all of this once seemed to me like a living death. I rebelled against their guidance, their persistent push toward bettering myself, embracing the often radically individualist, ruthlessly provocative punk subculture as my life preserver in a frighteningly stormy sea. Now, however, I hope to embody and pass on to my own son their gifts of love: my father's work ethic, his dedication to the underdog, and my mother's devotion to the needs of others, and the sense that gifts we receive are always meant to be shared.

This shift in perspective is revolutionary. Again, how amazing and, yes, humbling to realize that what I am doing for this little amazing life—all the drudgery, dirty diapers, sleepless nights, wrestling matches over clothes, food, and toys, and the often unspoken, but never-ending fears—this all was done for me, once upon a time. To paraphrase the mighty Nation of Ulysses, respect is due to all parents, especially my long-suffering ones.

Of course, to be humble enough to truly value our parents—accepting that we have become them in certain ways—doesn't mean we can't transcend their limitations, or learn from their mistakes, for surely we can, and must. Still, as we do this, we must also acknowledge that we build on the foundation they gave us, often at great cost to their own autonomy and desires.

Along the way, having found a certain peace with my parents and upbringing, I've come to understand the need to utilize both the past traditions and our future visions, in the proper proportion, to realize all that is possible. At the risk of seeming commonplace, I now aspire to put into action Reinhold Niebuhr's famous prayer for "the serenity of mind to accept that which cannot be changed; courage to change that which can be changed, and wisdom to know the one from the other"—all while knowing that I must revisit and reassess the balance in this equation, again and again.

In the end, I'd argue that the radical humility I am discovering as a father does not equate to surrendering to the-world-as-it-is. To the contrary, this quality is actually required to realize the process—not an event only—which might be called "revolution." This experience of mundane yet indispensable humanity gets us closer to the truth, that stubborn, unyielding bit of eternity that of course must be the foundation of any real transformation, any true effort to marshal the power of the people to build a new world.

This new understanding means that we see our old ideas in new light, sometimes refuting them, sometimes coming to a deeper understanding, one that makes them ever more relevant, even if in changed circumstances. We use pieces of all that we have been, all that we have seen, done, and believed, discarding what no longer seems to fit, but clutching close to us that which remains, that which still rings true.

From those shards we can create something new, something real, something all our own . . . something that can be part of that larger revolution for which we—and so much of our world—hungers.

That mission—from a father to a son, but through him to the world—is often made up of the magic of small moments. The little acts, the simple presence, a hug, a smile, the shared laughter, all of the glimpses of "living totally"—these are critical pieces of the everyday revolution. However humble, it is connected to the broader transformation, because it connects us to other people, to their lives, their dreams. Even if I don't know yet how to assemble all of the building blocks involved, or suspect I will never be able to fully live this insight, I know it to be true.

How then, to begin this journey, to march, skip, and sometimes trudge down its seemingly endless way? In the best punk sense, we do what we can with what we have, wherever we are right now . . . and we do it with one another, seeing ourselves as one family, finding power in our diversity as well as in our common humanity.

Today, I find myself in the once foreign land called fatherhood. Far from society's trap for the aging rebel, it has become a powerful new place to work, to struggle, to dream, to love . . . to be here to build a world that is as full, and challenging, and miraculous as the amazing youngster growing beautifully before my eyes.

To find myself a father to a son daily gives me more and more of the great gift of humility, of entering more deeply into and identifying with the human race, in all its beauty, folly, failure, and, yes, triumph. Now I know more than ever why I write, why I serve, why I struggle: it is for Soren, for all the children . . . and it is to pay the profound debt owed to my own parents, as I try in my way to carry on their dreams.

Inside vs. Outside
Jeremy Adam Smith

Once upon a time, I didn't know any parents my own age, but I'd see them on the streets with their young children.

I'd see the whining, the screaming, the messes, the rising frustration. I'd feel wings beating frantically against the walls of my chest, something fighting to escape. I'd think: *No, no, not me, never, parenthood looks horrible, they must be miserable.*

At that point in my life I expended a great deal of energy avoiding responsibility. I equated this absence with freedom.

After my wife Olli got pregnant, I would walk the streets of San Francisco with a feeling of doom, imagining—correctly—that I wouldn't be able to go there or do that after the baby came.

"The baby" was a very abstract concept.

Today I am a dad. Our son Liko sleeps in bed with us. At twenty-one months—two weeks ago—we started to night-wean him, so that he would not nurse all night on Olli. As I write, Olli sleeps in the living room; Liko and I sleep in the bedroom. We'll continue this arrangement until Liko no longer tries to nurse at night.

Why keep him in the bedroom at all? Why not just put him in a crib and close the door?

Because we don't want to. We like having him in bed with us. He'll get his own room someday. There's no rush. In the meantime, however, we don't want him pawing at Olli's breasts every hour on the hour from midnight till six a.m.

It's going fine. In the early months—the fabled fourth trimester—Liko needed Olli and in my ignorance and inexperience, I was largely a supportive bystander. I could not imagine putting him down to sleep without mom. I couldn't imagine caring for him all by myself, as a father. This bred a certain helplessness on my part, which I've been told is common to first-time fathers.

Last night as I watched Liko sleep, his little back rising and falling, something changed, as though I had been carrying within myself a message written in a language that I only at that moment learned to read. It's difficult to translate, from that inner language into English. I'll try.

Last night my son curled up into the crook of my arm. I held him, feeling like the bed was a raft and we were just drifting along some dark river. In a flash I felt totally responsible for Liko and totally capable of caring for him, day or night, in a way that I hadn't felt before.

That feeling of responsibility and capability gave me a concomitant feeling of confidence and power—not "power" in the sense of physical force or strength, but as in the ability to do what has to be done.

"Father" did not feel like a role that I was adopting, but like something intrinsic to my identity. It didn't feel "like" anything, really; it was its own thing, my thing, like my arms or my legs.

Today, as I write, I feel somehow more free than I have felt in two years. True, my world is smaller, baby-sized. But from where I now sit, I can see things that I've never seen before.

I am writing in the cafe of the San Francisco Main Public Library. A short time ago a young man, mid-twenties, sat down next to me with another young man, who suffers from a degenerative nervous disorder of some kind. They are strangers to me, but I have seen them both around the Mission many times, one caring for the other.

I don't know anything about their relationship—brothers, friends?

They both dress like Mission hipsters, in high-tops and thrift-store jackets, the kind of alterna-uniforms you see shoulder-to-shoulder at a Yo La Tengo concert. Over the years I've watched the sick one grow more palsied, more bent upon himself, less recognizable. I don't know anything about his illness, but I cannot imagine him surviving too many more years.

For the past fifteen minutes I covertly watched one hold a drink up to the other's mouth. I watched him wipe the other's chin, force the other's hands into a position that would allow him to eat, spoon food. A palsied hand knocked milk onto a shirt, the floor. One patiently cleaned it up. At the end one had a small seizure; the other dealt with it.

They just left, one guiding the other at the elbow. Watching them oppressed and saddened me; my hands feel heavy as I write. I'm trying to understand why. Part of the answer is that it is horrible to witness a dependency that can only end in death. But perhaps I was also seeing myself as I might appear with Liko to other people: burdened by responsibility, trapped in caring for another, covered in spit and milk. That's the external image.

Internally, how do the two young men feel? There must be anger, both at thwarted lives. But what freedom and power is there, where we can't see it?

If I could get into a time machine and find my childless old self sitting in a bar, knocking back his third beer, laughing with friends but secretly afraid of fatherhood, I might sidle up and whisper the truth: Parenthood is not what it seems. As a friend once told me, the life you're living will end, yes, but don't worry: you'll get a new life.

Glacial Crushing Joy
Mike Araujo

So many different feelings went through my mind when I first held my son, mostly shock mixed with concern that my partner was okay. He arrived with such clear eyes looking right at me; it was as though there was no place I could hide, my feelings were right there for him. I sat holding him as he quietly slept his first sleep on the planet, and I could only think of my father and how happy he would have been, and how gentle he actually was.

I grew up in a housing complex called Co-op City, the largest cooperative housing experiment in the country—very progressive, very open and optimistic—right there in the middle of the Bronx. It wasn't till many years later that I found out that it was supposedly a bad neighborhood. I saw it as a huge playground full of kids, up to sixty at a time, playing games like kick the can. For my parents, it was a refuge from the larger, colder, uglier world.

My mom and dad never told me why they moved to New York, but with hindsight I can see why: as an interracial couple it was dangerous for them in some places, illegal in others. In New York that wasn't an issue. My father was a worldly, retired professional boxer, a longshoreman and a painter who had met and painted with Picasso. My mother married young and was very Irish and very happy. They were so in love.

He seemed like a hero to me, powerful and smart, always making people laugh and think. He had all these crazy beatnik pals who would come around to mooch and joke. Mostly, though, I remember he worked, all the time. He would get home about the time I was going to school and he would take me down the elevator and walk me across the street to PS 160. I looked forward to that walk so much. Then he would pick me up for lunch and make something ridiculous with egg and linguiça.

On the weekend my mother and sister would hang out together, while me and my dad would go to the city and visit the galleries and museums. I would sit and look at the "knights in shining honor" and he would help me draw them. Then we would go to the pool halls and boxing gyms and shoot the shit with old-timers. I think these trips were more for him than me, and he would have these great arguments about boxing and art. I thought all fighters painted and all artists fought. Only later did I learn that the world can usually only see one thing at a time.

When I was older, we moved to Rhode Island, and it was so different. Before then I hadn't know that people lived in private houses; I thought that everyone lived in tiny apartments with parquet floors. I don't think I had seen rich people before. My dad got a job as a janitor at Brown University, still third-shift. He stopped having lunch with me—instead I just got the shitty assistance breakfast and lunch.

Pretty quickly I noticed something. The kids who lived in my housing project loved my dad, and they would ask him a million questions about boxing, and ask him to draw stuff. He always did even though he must have been so tired from work. But there was another group of kids who weren't from the project, who were from the fancy section of town—and we had to walk through that to get to and from my dad's studio. Those kids saw me with my dad. The next day at school those kids started in, saying how my dad cleaned toilets, which was true, and imitating how he walked, which was that toe step of a fighter. It was only the rich kids—the others knew my dad. But I felt so small.

I ran home crying and I'm ashamed to say I told my dad I wish we had never moved, and I said that if we stayed in the Bronx this wouldn't have happened. I blamed him. He didn't say a word. We just walked silently to his studio. Everything seemed different.

So much happens after you turn twelve. Everything is so important; all decisions are life or death. You spend your adolescent years lurching from crisis to crisis. It is all about you, despite the words and intentions you simply live for yourself as a teenager. Punk rock, skateboards, beer, and friends were everything, and I couldn't see past my own navel.

Strange things started to happen to my dad. He would forget things, leave burners on—he was even late for work once, and once he went in on the wrong day. My mother was growing increasingly irritable at what she thought was my dad's absent-mindedness. Everything was tense. I took refuge in my friends, in the process becoming an unpleasant little punk. I stayed away from home and couldn't help but get arrested. I was a bad kid. My sister had moved out. I didn't once think of what my mother must have been going through. Nice kid.

An illness like the one my father had is so cruel. It's not a shock; it's a creeping decay that grinds you down. Over and over you have to do the same thing, a glacial crushing of joy. Every time I went out with him, I was terrified of what would happen. The worst part was the whispers. He was a well-known athlete in Rhode Island and folks loved him, but now when they saw him they accused him of being "punch-drunk." But he was a champion. He hit people; he didn't get hit.

My dad had to stay home more often and the union covered his shifts. We would be home together, but it felt like prison. Once we were sitting, not saying a word, and I smelled something, something bad. My dad had shit himself. I was furious. I had plans, after all, and changing my dad's diapers was not part of them. I took him to the shower, stripped him, took off the dirty diaper... I think it was the first time I had really looked at him. He seemed so small and frail, not the man I knew, even though it was. I started sobbing, and all my *affect*—the hair, the airs, the attitude—it all seemed so fucking stupid. My dad stood there shivering and I cried, because I didn't know what to do. I just held him.

In the thirteen years since the death of my father, I have really spent a lot of time reliving my petty impatience and irritation, and suffering a lot of guilt. I spent so much time denying my identity as a caregiver. I was thinking like a man for whom work, money, effort pushed in every direction except the one that leads you closer to each other, closer to your own self. The nurturing that I did I did with a great deal of complaint, but I did it.

When my son Xavier showed himself to me, I saw this new person wholly dependent, but individual. He couldn't talk to me and I had to guess, I had to *infer* his needs. I think that day in the bathroom with my father is the day that I let my whole self be available, that I became ready for fatherhood. The attrition of the illness had simply worn me down, but also showed me *how*. Xavier was going to get that man, me, as his father. I would try to be as complete to him as I could be. I shared my life, totally. I have no expectation beyond what I can offer now. What I offer is my love and my humanity. I love you, Xavier George Brown Araujo.

A Day at the Park
Shawn Taylor

1. I'm unsure why, but I get asked—quite often—about the hardest part of being a father. The people who ask me this are almost all younger cats who are about to become fathers or are there already. That question is a Pandora's box. Being a father is hard in a million different ways: balancing fatherhood with partnership; being able to do the things that I love to do on a consistent basis (for example, writing—I'm writing this at 3 a.m., while everyone is asleep and I have a moment to myself); the loss of money; having to send your child to childcare because both parents have to work to afford all the additional costs. Working all day, coming home at night and only seeing your child for forty-five minutes before their bedtime—in these ways and more, daddyhood is hard as hell. But none of this (yes, even the money problems) even comes close to the raging difficulty of being a father of color.

2. Being tattooed, visually Black (I'm half Jamaican and half Puerto Rican), over six feet tall and muscular, holding a little ethnically-ambiguous toddler makes many people double, triple, quadruple take—and also, for some odd reason, loosens tongues, mostly of white folks, and creates an environment of familiarity. And yet they still manage to see me wrong: In my daughter's twenty-two months of living, I have been labeled "uncle," "babysitter," "guardian," "cousin," but never father. I can't tell you just how crushing a blow this is. I *love* being a father and I think that I am becoming a better one by the day, but to have one of my greatest joys discounted is painful.

3. Do we really live in a society that is still stuck in the lie that Black men cannot be fathers? Well . . . I must admit that I was on that same shit for a while. When my partner told me she was pregnant, I had fears that, at the moment of birth, a Greyhound

ticket would appear in my hands and I'd leave my partner and new child to fend for themselves. I thought I'd become an absent father sleeper agent—the baby's first cry would activate me and my mission would be to get as far away from mother and baby as possible. Because, throughout my whole childhood, I never once had a friend or met anyone (of color) whose father lived with them, or in some cases, even knew who their fathers were. There is a generation of brothers and sisters born after Viet Nam and before the release of *Ghostbusters* that are a tribe of fatherless children. My own father, I saw the bastard five times in my life.

4. People mistaking me for everything but being a father almost invariably happens at the playground. While the mothers (rarely do I see fathers at the playgrounds) are sitting in groups, either texter-bating or focusing intently on some new piece of thousand-dollar baby gadget—I'm in the sand, on the structure, kicking the ball. I'm playing with my kid. Over at this park in El Cerrito, California, I was teaching my daughter how to hang from one of the monkey bars. She is a ridiculously daring kid and will try anything, as long as it is dangerous. This kindly older woman (dressed up like a fashion model to go the park) smiled at me and said, "My uncle used to do the same thing for me. He always let me do the things that my father would never let me do." She drew out the "never" as if I was tossing my daughter over an open lion's mouth. I told this woman that I was an only child, that my kid didn't have any uncles, and that I was her father. She glanced between my daughter and me several times, and finally said, "Noooooo." Wow.

5. When I think about it more, not being recognized or acknowledged as my daughter's father, while painful, isn't nearly as crazy as being a man-of-color at a park. When race, size, gender, and how we dress intersect, it disrupts social fabrics. Like I stated earlier, I play with my kid while at the playground. And if my daughter decides to play with other kids, I play with them too. I don't touch them, because you just don't do that—you don't touch other people's kids without permission. One day I was kicking a soccer ball with my daughter and some other little kids. One of the kids, a little girl, tripped, fell down, and scraped her cheek on the wood that bordered the play area. I helped her to her feet and asked her if she was OK. She looked over at her mother, who was starting intently at her cellular phone, and got nothing. She then looked at

me, I looked at her, and she wailed as though the end of the world was nigh. The cellular mom looked up, fixed me with the most baleful stare, and ran over to us, dialing her phone. Instead of asking her daughter if she was OK, she snatched her up by the arm and thrust her behind her back. I then heard her telling her husband, "This big nigger just pushed Miriam to the ground." Unbelievable.

6. I gathered our things, and made to leave. This lady then blocked our way. "You can attack a kid, but now that my husband is coming you're trying to leave? You're not going anywhere." She then put her hand on my arm and tried to stop us. All the while my daughter is getting freaked out because she is very rarely exposed to yelling or overt signs of anger. Being who I am, I figured, "Let's see how this plays out."

7. Three minutes later, an SUV pulls up and this really fit dude pops out of the truck and comes barreling towards us. I see that he has his fist cocked a little. I put my daughter down and sent her to go and play, which she was grateful for. I could feel just how tense and anxious she became. This guy came up and started screaming at me. Before fatherhood, I would have gone at him, but I have been trying to change that part of myself; violence is a social ingredient that I am weaning myself from. When he finally paused, I asked him did he think that yelling and threatening me was going to do any good? I then asked him why neither he nor his wife had asked Miriam what had happened. I then asked them, "If I were a white dude, would you still think that I pushed your daughter?" That stopped them. All this time that the silly adults are going at it, little Miriam is clinging to her mother's legs, terrified. "Your daughter fell, and I helped her up." I focused on the mother: "And if you weren't so busy looking at your phone, if you were actually parenting, you would have seen what happened. Better yet, it might not have even happened if you were playing with us." Then I looked at the dad: "I can appreciate your concern, but if this is how you react to situations you know nothing about, you might get hurt. If this was two years ago, I would have beat the shit out of you for yelling in my face and pretending like you were going to do something." I then bent down and asked Miriam if she was OK. She looked at her parents, and then at me, and nodded. I took out a wipe and wiped her scraped cheek. "Does it feel better now?" She nodded. I gave her dad the dirty wipe, and went to go and play with my daughter.

8. That encounter still nags at me on a number of different levels. Miriam's parents never answered my question: If I were white, would they still have accused me of hurting their daughter? My honor as a father and as a human being had been totally disregarded. Two children had to experience the stupidity of their elders: Miriam's parents for false accusations and racist words, and me for delivering veiled threats. I lost that day. I lost the core of the person who I am trying to become. I lost hope that my daughter would be able to live in a world where skin color wasn't a factor. I lost faith that the rift between white and black folks could ever be repaired.

9. As we were driving home, I started to cry. It came up and spilled out so powerfully that I had to pull the car over, turn it off, and just let everything come: Not having a father of my own to ask if he had to deal with anything similar; almost dipping into self-hatred because of my skin color; cursing so many men that came before me for fucking it up for my generation; every nigger I have been and would be called; how my daughter's hair is different than her parent's and how people point out this difference as if my kid had won the lotto. All this was trapped in my crying. I saw my daughter through the rearview mirror and she looked so sad and scared that I had to hold her. I pulled over, got her out of her car seat, and we sat on the hood of the car, holding each other. I cried into her hair and she, feeling daddy's energy, cried into my chest. We were there for a little while when this old woman hobbled by and smiled at us. "You have such a beautiful daughter," this woman said. "She has your eyes."

Mommy Preference and Patriarchy
David L. Hoyt

"The first crying of children is a prayer . . . They begin by asking
our aid; then end by compelling us to serve them. Thus from
their very weakness, whence comes, at first, their feeling of de-
pendence, springs afterwards the idea of empire, and of com-
manding others."
—Jean-Jacques Rousseau, *Émile; or, Concerning Education*

In our family, I take care of the home and my wife takes care of
the money. But when my wife took a long vacation from work so
we could all spend more time together, our family went through a
strange regression. At the end of this transition, I had emerged as
a slothful Patriarch, presiding over a career-woman-turned-harried
housewife, who was herself now answering to every beck and call
of an infantilized preschooler.

Our family had become, in other words, the opposite of what
it had been before my wife took her sabbatical.

The transformation was driven by our son, who quickly re-
vealed himself to be a rogue monkey with every intention of completely overturning the social hierarchy. It began when he demonstrated a strong preference for Mama during her first week or two
at home. At first, this made perfect sense to me: Mama is a working woman and Spot doesn't get to spend as much time with her
as with me. I was sympathetic, since I liked having her around, too.

But I had no idea that this shared desire, as expressed by my
son, would launch our family unit into an unwitting sociological
experiment, the sort of thing that might have been inflicted by
scientists on hapless and undeserving primates in the 1950s, or by
media execs on equally hapless but much more deserving humans
on a reality TV show.

Falling to the bottom of the social ladder, though shocking, was not necessarily new to me. It had happened in catastrophic fashion at the beginning of seventh grade, and thereafter with smaller aftershocks in the years leading up to college. So although I wasn't emotionally devastated as I had been in seventh grade, I recognized what was happening. I was getting pushed to the bottom of the pack hierarchy. Lower than Grandpa, maybe even lower than my brother-in-law, and probably about on par with the dog. I was denied high-fives and daddy-hugs. I was bummed.

This was disturbing, of course. It was an injury to my self-love. Or so I thought, until I realized that in truth it heralded my liberation. For, as I was being spurned, my wife was being enslaved. She was shackled by Spot's preference for Mama. And for the first time in nearly four years, vistas of freedom opened up before me, of Rabbits running on Updike-like getaways, or of simpler, more local bouts of laziness. It was my one and only chance, in the artificial circumstances of my wife's sabbatical, to don the mantle of paterfamilias, Patriarch, Godfather, master of the kinship clan.

I can't say that I hadn't been warned. Weeks before I had descended the staircase one morning. In a bath of soft light before me I saw the heartwarming scene of a mother, dressed for work and feeding breakfast to her son, holding a boy in a puppy-covered sleeper with puppy ears flopping off the side of each foot. Yet this boy, shattering the Norman Rockwell charm of the scene, frowned when he saw me, and raised an accusatory, pointed finger into the air.

"Daddy, you go back upstairs!"

Although he had since learned to sheath the knife of this raw Oedipal hatred, he immediately took advantage of Mama's sabbatical to demand her services not just for breakfast, but for dinner as well. "I want Mama!" became not just a breakfast demand, but a cry uttered to ward off Daddy whenever he approached. But this preference soon turned into imperialism. Mama had to be the one to draw the bath and wash him. Mama had to help him with the potty. Mama had to brush his teeth. Mama had to carry all thirty-seven pounds of him up two flights of stairs. Mama had to come sit with him on the couch for yet another episode of *Ni Hao, Kai-lan*. Mama had to handle every case of crisis management.

Spot's relationship with his Mama has always had this potential to regress towards infantile dependency. This doesn't surprise me, since I had the same problem with women well into my twenties. But now it was evolving into sheer despotism, something I had never managed to achieve. I realized this when Spot began *telling*—not asking—Mama to pick up little things that had fallen off the couch and onto the floor. When Spot began saying things like, "Mama, I want *you* to pick up the block!" that was six inches away, we both knew it was time for her to go back to work. In the meantime, there was nothing for me to do but lie back on the couch, pop the button on my jeans, and flip on the game. Aside from being on-call as in-house Bad Cop, my time was now my own.

I thought I might finish all sorts of projects, paint a few rooms, and get started on the novel I've been meaning to write for twenty years. In reality, seeing the hours and days of my wife's sabbatical consumed in the service of a tyrant marooned me with guilt. I couldn't help her—Spot wouldn't let me—and I got nothing done for myself. Looking back, I can't say that Mama's sabbatical was relaxing, or that my temporary position as default patriarch was terribly satisfying. But we were all together more often than usual, and we wound up packing quite a lot of activity into that one summer month. Looking back on that time now gives me the pleasant feeling of having richly lived.

So what does it all mean? Short answer: All is flux. The lust for power resides within us all. Patriarchy is really not all that enjoyable if you like an emotionally engaged relationship with your child and have any respect for your partner.

Long answer: Emotions don't obey contracts, not even 50/50 coparenting contracts, or more exotic reverse-traditional ones. They ebb and flow and shift around, collecting around one person for a while before melting away and collecting more closely around someone else. Spot's shift in preference was only as abrupt and extreme as the sudden change in our domestic routines. And by the end of Mama's sabbatical, his attachments had begun to even out again. He let me carry him, and we picked up some of our exclusive father-son routines again. My brief stint as Patriarch, as close to the real thing as a weekend reenactment is to the Battle of Gettysburg, was nonetheless close enough to reassure me that such a role was not for me.

Spot clearly has a different relationship with both of us, tending ever so slightly towards dependency with Mama, and ever so slightly towards imitation and competition with Daddy. But there is plenty of dependency on Daddy, and some imitation of Mama, too. So I really can't say with any confidence that our particular arrangement has affected Spot's emotional preferences one way or another, or that he will "bond" with either of us because one of us happens to leave the house in the morning while the other does not.

It is with Spot's emotional attachments as it is with subatomic particles: the likelihood that they will be there over the long run is more certain than the existence of a singular, passionate attachment at any one point in time. A few months of breastfeeding in infancy, or one ten-day fishing trip in adolescence are probably not, in my opinion, enough to guarantee a bond one way or another over the course of a lifetime. The hours, days, and years of effort made to sustain the existence and happiness of someone else stand a far better chance of doing so.

This is something I remind myself during those stretches when I am not the "favored" parent, and—when I'm not feeling like a favored spouse—something that probably applies to marriage as well.

My Daddy Is Transgendered!
Jack Amoureux

I didn't have plans to be a parent and I really didn't have plans to be a dad. All of this quickly changed when, just over a year ago, I came out as transgendered—and not too long after began dating my current partner, Angela, who was then three months pregnant and a single mother-to-be by choice. For me, the process of becoming a parent has been closely intertwined with the process of rethinking what gender means to me, and with the process of figuring out whether my girlfriend could be my life partner.

My partner and I are now on the sixth month of our journey into parenthood. Talking about it abstractly, if I told you that we have a queer family, you might not believe me. Our baby has a mom (Angela) and a dad (me). Yet, Angela identifies as queer and I identify as transgendered or gender queer, use male pronouns and (as of now) do not want to physically "transition." For me, gender is a continuum, and I lie somewhere on the male end of the spectrum, but that doesn't change my sexuality. I am a homo.

As a family *out* in this world, literally and figuratively, this sometimes makes for a lot of confusion. The gay boy at the grocery store we frequent refers to us "moms." I often get weird looks when just Ocean and I are out in public. With my youthful and boyish appearance people seem to wonder what a fifteen-year-old is doing with an infant.

Even friends and family often seem confused. Some either completely avoid using a parental moniker for me, or they awkwardly pause before a strained "Daddy," or they ask, "So, what are you going by these days?" My partner's mom, when talking to Ocean, often refers to us as "Mom and Jack" and frequently uses female pronouns for me. This is not to say that everyone gets it wrong or is weird about our parental roles and my gender identity.

It feels wonderful and affirming when my friend, Jen, refers to me as "Daddy" in her baby talk with Ocean.

Still, I can't entirely attribute all of this confusion and ambiguity to my gender identity. It also has to do with the fact that while Ocean is growing up and we are actively parenting her, Angela and I are also trying to figure out our relationship to each other and to Ocean. The questions we have encountered and struggled with include: When do we go from dating to partnership to life partnership? What marks that? When does Angela go from a single parent to a coparent? When do I move from parenting to be being an equal coparent? We're not undertaking this process in a "normal" way—dating, partnering, and then having a kid together.

The difficulty of these questions was magnified by the emotion involved in what we were practicing every minute of every day—parenting. It was hard to be up with Ocean several times a night, laugh and play with her every day, make parenting decisions with Angela, and then hear a good friend identify Ocean as belonging to just Angela at a party.

Fortunately, things seem more settled now, but perhaps not in ways that we anticipated. For one, we found that instead of figuring out our relationship first and then, based on that, deciding my parental status, didn't work for us. We're very optimistic but we're not entirely sure that we'll be life partners. We're just not there yet. But I'm definitely Ocean's parent. I will always be her papa.

Also, I didn't expect that it would be so difficult for Ocean to have a mom and a dad. And not just for Angela, but for me too. When Angela is talking to someone who doesn't know us and refers to her partner as "he" and "dad," it doesn't resonate with either of our senses of queer identity and how we thought our everyday sexual politics would play out. When Ocean goes to school she'll talk of a mom and dad, not two moms or two dads. I know that these situations are more awkward for Angela and this makes me feel sad. When I talk about Angela or my kid, it's different. People almost always read me as queer, whether as a trannie or a butch woman. I still don't know what to do with this.

What has clearly emerged is that one of the major challenges for us has been crafting a family that accords with the politics we hold around sexual and gender identity. We want to refer to each other and talk about each other in a way that feels queer.

Fortunately, we're beginning to find some good models. For example, we have an acquaintance who is a transgendered parent and his kid goes around saying, "My daddy is transgendered!" This gives us hope that Ocean can also grow up, in her own way, knowing that we're not a heterosexual family and expressing that openly, even if it makes for a tense moment when we're visiting my family in Idaho and hanging out on the gun range.

Identifying as transgendered is important to me. It just feels right when Angela, my friends and my colleagues refer to me as "he." I don't want to be "stealth"—to always and unequivocally pass as male. This is important for many transgendered persons, but not for me. I have decided to stake out a gender identity somewhere outside of the dichotomous framework that most people hold because it is how I view gender conceptually and how I view my own gender. I feel strongly that this is an important political project. I work in a field that is not always friendly to this way of thinking about gender. I am completing my Ph.D. in International Relations and one of my advisors who is a lesbian has urged me not to use male pronouns in going out on the job market. I am also on the board of directors of an organization of military families (Military Families Speak Out) and made the decision when I was nominated to present myself as transgendered. And when I talk about being a parent, that lets others know that transgendered persons have families too and it is important to recognize and protect them.

I am sure that presenting myself as transgendered in all of these ways is a positive thing, for me and for our queer communities. But I'm not sure that it will always have positive consequences for my family. As a transgendered person will I get a job? Not because I'm a guy and thus I need to be the "breadwinner" and support my family, but because at least one of us needs a decent job in tough economic times. Will my kid get beat up for having a transgendered dad? And how will Angela and I find a way to sustain our family in a way that affirms both our parental roles and our status as queers?

I think we're beginning to find answers to these questions. One thing is certain, Ocean makes it worth it. Amongst the nighttime feedings and the moments of fussiness are the things that make parenthood and having a family exhilarating: Ocean's smiles and giggles when we get home, her wide-eyed and bushy-tailed disposition at seven in the morning that makes it hard to be grumpy and tired, family snuggle time on the couch, pushing Ocean around the house on a skateboard, showing off Ocean at a party full of queers, and dropping Ocean off for a few hours on a Saturday afternoon so that Angela and I can have sex. It seems that this is what queer family is about.

Upside-Down Lucas
Burke Stansbury

When Krista and I started talking about having a child to-gether I couldn't help imagining the cool stuff we would someday all do together. Conversations about the future are es-pecially a favorite for Krista, and in the early months of her preg-nancy, as we traveled around El Salvador and Colombia, she would think aloud about us crisscrossing Latin America as a family, or trekking in the mountains of the Pacific Northwest where we both grew up, or riding bikes along urban trails in whatever city we someday ended up in.

For me, I couldn't get a certain archetype image out of my head: that of tossing the football or shooting hoops with my young child, teaching her or him how to play the sports that infatuated me when I was growing up. And then there was our shared com-mitment to political organizing and activism. Krista and I celebrat-ed our child's first direct-action protest—albeit still in the womb—when we both played key roles in a street shutdown in front of the White House while Krista was five months pregnant.

Then Lucas was born. In the months after his harrowing premature birth, we sat in the neonatal intensive care unit of Children's Hospital and watched these dreams slowly slip away. Lucas was finally released from the hospital after three months, and then admitted again two months later, at which point he re-ceived the diagnosis we had been dreading—a severe neuromuscu-lar disorder called myotubular myopathy.

Though the diagnosis was painfully drawn out, and though we experienced some extremely low emotional moments along the way, Krista and I ultimately came to terms with Lucas's disabil-ity probably quicker than most parents of special-needs kids. Our commitment to social justice work gave us a framework to think about the structural conditions that lead people with disabilities to be excluded from many aspects of our society. Lucaș was a beautiful, happy little baby, and I felt confident that we would fight to create a world where children like him could in fact participate, despite their physical limitations.

While he was still a baby it was easy to idealize this framework. Babies spend most of their time in the crib or lying around on the floor anyway, right? But in the months around his first birthday Lucas's rapid growth was astonishing. Sometimes we would wake up and go to give Lucas a morning kiss in his crib and it would seem as if he'd added another half inch during the night. By the time he hit eighteen months he had basically grown out of his second crib—there was only an inch of space left before both his feet and the top of his head were touching the ends.

Some parents would brag about such a feat, but Lucas's height is a cause for alarm. People know that Lucas has a disease—the fact that he has a tracheotomy to help him breathe and is connected to a ventilator much of the day makes it obvious—but they don't necessarily realize what his rapid growth rate means for him and for us as time goes on. Lucas can't sit up or move his body much at all. While his fine motor skills have developed remarkably, he is virtually unable to twist his torso, shift body positions, or roll over.

Under these circumstances, Lucas's rate of growth isn't all that exciting; rather, it's downright scary, especially when we once again begin imagining ourselves with an adolescent child. No hiking and limited travel. We can participate in a protest rally as a family only under very special circumstances. And then there's the physicality of his predicament: the taller Lucas gets the more chance he'll have of developing scoliosis later in life; the longer his torso gets, the quicker he grows out of his special braces and chair, meaning that he needs new ones. And the weight gain makes it increasingly hard to move Lucas around.

Myotubular myopathy causes Lucas's overall "muscle tone"—the resting state of muscles—to be so low that handling him is like lifting a floppy rag doll. Picking Lucas up is a complicated ordeal. When you put a single hand under his waist and lift, his butt goes up but the rest of his body stays on the ground. His arms fall back behind him, his legs droop, and if you don't have the other hand firmly behind his neck, then you're in big trouble. The ventilator tubing connected to his trach and the pulse-ox monitor probe running from his toe compounds all of this, adding an extra layer to an already challenging maneuver.

And yet, lifting Lucas is not only necessary but often a total joy: when Lucas is in a good mood there's nothing he enjoys more than getting swung around the room, or having his head flipped back into "upside-down Lucas" position, or laying on someone's chest for a good snuggle session. It wasn't long ago that we could easily pick Lucas up and do all this stuff, and we can still pull it off, but twenty-five pounds of a very floppy body is different than fifteen pounds. And it's hard to imagine thirty-five pounds. Or fifty.

There's not much we can do about Lucas growing. He's not chubby and we're certainly not going to starve him. In general, being tall is a characteristic of people with myotubular myopathy, one of those freaky things about this disease that seems to doubly punish kids like Lucas: not only is this genetic mutation going to dramatically inhibit the development of your muscles, but it's going to make your body really long as well so that moving around is that much more difficult. Lucas likely will never be able to walk, and he probably won't be able to sit up straight on his own anytime soon. Playing with him in the ways we now do will get more challenging as he grows. Moving him from place to place is also going to get a lot harder.

Still, I am awed by our son's strength in the face of his physical weakness. There are so many amazing things that he's doing these days that usually Krista and I can't help but focus on the positive: when he's cracking up because someone is about to raspberry his tummy, when he's exploring a fascinating new toy and deliberating on how to best get it into his mouth, or when he's splashing his legs around in his undersized bathtub. With Lucas, patience is a virtue. The more time you spend with him and allow him to do his thing, the more remarkable he becomes.

With the help of therapists we've invented new toys and games better suited for Lucas given his low muscle tone, and I love the creative challenge of coming up with the perfect Lucas plaything for his current stage of development. We also think about changing certain life practices to keep up with Lucas. I commit to stretching my back more, strengthening my abdominal muscles, and even starting to hit the weight room for the first time since high school. Lately I've been joking that I'll have to get a personal trainer soon in order to get all of my Lucas-lifting muscles in better shape.

Yet these are practical things that don't actually get at the emotional rollercoaster that is parenting a medically fragile child like Lucas. We can be creative and flexible in ways the incorporate Lucas into many aspects of daily life, while also delving into the world of disability rights so as to challenge our society to better accommodate children like Lucas. But the visions of our family hiking in the mountains or of me playing basketball with my son will never go away. Nor do the images of other typically developing kids running around the grocery store or climbing trees in the park. As much as we love Lucas as he is, we won't ever be able to forget that cruel twist, that tiny modification in his genes, which prevents him from doing much of what human beings enjoy about life. So despite having a strong partner in Krista, and an amazing support network of family and friends, and an empowering framework of disability justice, I still cry sometimes when I think about Lucas's future.

Its scary to think that every pound Lucas gains and every half inch he adds to his height gets us a little closer to that day when it won't be so easy to pick him up and dance around the room. Because dancing around makes Lucas happy. And so does cruising on the make-believe choo-choo train that is my knee, not to mention pushing his head back when he's in my arms—sometimes dozens of times a day—so that I'll flip him into "upside-down Lucas" position. At these moments seeing his face light up in a smile, and his hand wag in the sign for "more" is about the best thing I could ever imagine. So we'll cherish each minute and imagine, sometimes anxiously, new adventures that he can take part in even as he grows bigger.

How *Not* to Talk to Your Kid about War
Jeremy Adam Smith

*S*cene: *A San Francisco restaurant. Liko is two years old and he's eating pasta.*

Me: Liko, do you want to go to the antiwar protest tomorrow?

Liko (mouth full): What's an antiwar?

Me: In an antiwar protest, people get together and they ask war to stop.

Liko (he swallows): Why?

Me: Remember what we talked about yesterday? War is really terrible. Mommies and daddies and little kids like you get hurt really bad; sometimes they get killed.

Liko: Where is the war?

Me: Tomorrow we are going to protest the war in Iraq.

Liko: Where is Iraq?

Me: I showed you yesterday on the globe. It's very far from here. The people there don't speak our language or dress like us, but they're people just like us and they don't like to get hurt.

Liko: Are we going to get dessert?

Me: I don't think so.

Liko: Why?

Me: Because you already had ice cream today. Do you want to go to the antiwar protest?

Liko: I want to be a war-guy and hurt people!

Me (flustered): What? We don't want to hurt people, Liko. We want to help them.

Liko (bashes table with his hand): I want a war-stick! [Meaning a gun.]

Me: Liko, please don't hit the table.

Liko: Why?

Me: Because we're in a restaurant and we don't hit tables.

Liko: Why?

Me: Because it bothers the people around us.

Liko (looking around): Are those people going to the antiwar protest?

Me (glancing around and feeling slightly defeated): Some of them might, sure.

Liko: What do people do at an antiwar protest?

Me: We march and sing songs and hold signs.

Liko: What do the signs say?

Me: They say things like "Stop the war" or "War is bad for children."

Liko: I want to make a sign.

Me: OK. What should it say?

Liko: No hitting!

Section Two

CHILDHOOD

Beautiful on All Sides
Tomas Moniz

"And finally this, when the sun was falling down so beautiful we
didn't have time to give it a name, she held the child born of a
white mother and a red father and said, 'both sides of this baby
are beautiful.'" —Sherman Alexie

My youngest daughter wants to be white.
Or that's my fear. What I really should say is that my
youngest daughter has entered the stage of seeing ethnicity for
what it is—socially constructed symbols of meaning, ways of in-
clusion and exclusion; she now actively looks to associate things
with ethnicity.

"Why is it that those cars always play loud music?"

I wanna blame it on her schooling, on the media, but that's
a cop-out on my part. Because I have in fact actively helped her
to see ethnicity, to not be afraid to talk about ethnicity, and so by
implication encouraged her to begin her own process of situating
herself along a cultural spectrum. But now she's choosing her own
connections, aligning herself with what I personally have worked
to be critical of: whiteness. And it's my fault. I have shared with
her my own difficulties being bicultural as well as my own realiza-
tions about how ethnicity is connected to power, privilege, class.
But somehow I assumed that because I have been so sensitive to
and critical of whiteness and its privileges (even as I tried to recognize those issues in my life), my daughter would somehow be
critical of it as well. And yet maybe she is being critical, and she is
simply making her own decisions about these issues, forcing me
to consider the difficulties of supporting your children when their
decisions run counter to your own.

*"I think graffiti makes things look ugly and I don't know why they
do it."*

Let me explain. My son sees himself as a mix; he's searching for connections in things I searched for meaning in. He's aligning himself with politics and art in similar ways: hip-hop, the Zapatistas, the fashion of the young urban male. I understand how he feels pulled to these things as I was fifteen years ago, and I also see him struggle with the ways he doesn't fit those stereotypes that he's been indoctrinated with. I hope it leads him to an understanding that we must "make our familia from scratch," like Cherrie Moraga says. That we can create ourselves in the images we can imagine. For him, being a man can mean so many things besides what our culture wants to prescribe: silent, violent, angry, doing drugs, homophobic. I try to model other options, other forms of manhood, as do the other men in our lives: my brothers and my cousins. But my son sees my father in jail, my uncles in jail, he sees friend after friend choosing to experiment with drugs and violence. He understands that to be a young man, you need to be bad. I did too at one time, but I survived. I believe he can as well.

My middle daughter seems to lean towards that path as well, but she's the silent one, the one that keeps to herself. The one who seems totally immune to peer pressure, dresses the way she wants, chooses to be by herself sometimes; at other times, she's just one in the group of girls running the streets of south Berkeley. She reads and draws voraciously. She's fascinated by Frida Kahlo, enjoys Le Tigre, talks to complete strangers at the anarchist book fair, selling copies of *Rad Dad* for me. She just seems rooted in herself, and yet flexible enough to own so many different aspects of her identity. And because she's brown, the one with darker skin, darker hair, darker features, I tend to believe she sees herself as a comfortable *mestizaje*, the blend of her mother and father: a Jewish, Russian, Chicana, gringa. And she's proud of it all.

But Ella, my youngest, is light. Ella sees the struggles her mother and I have with our son and his associations with urban male culture; she sees my son's attempt to connect with certain things and so she is choosing the other path. I think she is seeing herself as white since it seems less complex than the choices I or her brother have made. Plus, she sees whiteness all around her in the media: fair skinned, blondish hair, light eyes. She sees herself in society's images. What can I do?

"Dad, you look Mexican, but I look white."

I don't know how to respond to her when she says that. Now I know my daughter, and this is her way of asking questions and, more importantly, beginning to individuate from me and her older sister and brother, with whom she tends to polarize. So she likes houses in the hills, hates graffiti and hip-hop, wants to dress properly, wants to follow the rules. She is incredibly perceptive, and she's aware that it's about ethnicity and class in those ways kids know and can allude to if not out right question.

"Why can't everyone live in north Berkeley, if it's this nice?"

She is the one who has aligned herself with the more mainstream qualities of our society. I feel my job is to not answer her or try to teach her, but to probe, question, help her see the difficulty in such static definitions without making her uncomfortable around the issue of ethnicity, as so many people are. I think she has seen me struggle to identify ethnicity and privilege. As a father I have taken her to countless meetings and events in the radical community. She has heard and listened to conversations about identity politics and sexual politics; I've asked questions of her and her sister about things they see. Although I know it's not completely analogous, a recent instance at this year's anarchist café brought up similar feelings. A person comes up to the food line wearing a teddy and hair clips with lots of make up and big hoop earrings. The person has that androgynous look as well as those contradictory gender cues that signal male and female. I see Ella looking, taking it in, the voice, the movements, the physical clues. She sees me looking at her.

"I wonder if that's a boy or a girl."

"Hmm, well, why does it have to be one or the other?"

She smiles and already has a response to me.

"Well, I think it is a bgirl."

We laugh, and I say it certainly might be, but I see her staring. She wants to know not what it might be if we lived in a world where gender was a choice, was fluid, could blend. She wants to know now, in her world, what things are.

Ethnicity is pervasive in our society as is the silence around it. I hate the privilege of whiteness to act as if ethnicity is passé, that when someone brings up ethnicity they are playing the "race" card. That is the ultimate in "racial" privilege. But I can't really have this conversation with my eight-year-old daughter when she asks me.

"Why is it that boys get into trouble in school more than girls, especially the black boys?"

Do I launch into a diatribe against teachers who privilege certain learning styles, who enter the classroom predisposed to see young boys of color as problems? She has learned her lessons of ethnicity well, from me as well as from this racist culture we live. If you claim a color or if you are seen by your color, you get noticed, usually in bad ways. Why shouldn't she choose to blend? In our family where ethnicity is always visible, even as we struggle to identify with it, to associate it, she sees clearly a road with less struggle, an easier road than what our son is trying to traverse.

It's of course ironic, some form of karmic retribution. For me as a child and teenager, living with my white mom, I was always too white to be Mexican, too brown to be white. And as an adult who has identified with my Chicano history and worked to understand my bicultural sense of self, passing has always been the bane of my existence. In this U.S. culture race is fixed, static—you're black or Mexican or Asian. And for white folks, U.S. culture (read: whiteness) refuses to see itself, and instead, white folks tend to buy into the belief in the universal, which of course is whiteness; that's the privilege of being white in the U.S.—you don't have to see it.

But for a growing majority of people, ethnicity is fluid; it's piecemeal, chosen, reclaimed, refused, relearned. There is a danger of appropriation; there is a need to be clear on intent and responsibility; there is a need for dialog, lots of it. I guess as my daughter brings up again and again ethnicity, I should relish the opportunity to talk about it. As we read stories and look at the pictures: *Oh, she has hair like mine, I wanna be her.* In the media: *Why does the donkey from* Shrek *sound black?* In our family: *Dad, how come grandma stopped calling you Tomas?* In how we each define ourselves.

As parents, that is our struggle: to be honest, even when it is scary. To be truthful, even when it weighs heavy on our shoulders, when it might hurt, when it implicates us, our choices, our past, perhaps our future. We need to be willing to be open, direct, to call out racism when we see it, but be willing to listen to ideas and experiences from our kids as they begin to see, test, choose identities different from our own. I have wanted to protect my kids, wanted to give them a history that embraced all aspects of their identities in positive, powerful ways. I wanted to create an environment where ethnicity was so visible that it lost its meaning, and we became who we wanted to be, not limited by definitions but not a nebulous attempt at universality. We are and aren't things. Learn, choose, be accountable. But perhaps it is me that needs to relearn and trust, to step back and see how we can be white and brown; we can even be bgirls or gboys all at the same time.

Mixed Dominance
Jeremy Adam Smith

My son Liko has one developmental issue. It's usually called mixed dominance, but you can also call it cross-dominance, mixed-handedness, mixed laterality, or hand-confusion—genuine ambidexterity is a rare manifestation of mixed dominance. In Liko's case, this means, for example, that right now he tends to eat with his right hand but draw with his left.

Is this truly an issue? He may very well be ambidextrous; he may gradually end up favoring one hand. We're seeing an occupational therapist to sort it out, but I'm not terrifically worried.

Indeed, neither his mother nor I are surprised that our son tries to have it both ways: mixed dominance defines Liko's life, on so many levels.

In infancy and toddlerhood, most folks thought my boy was a girl, and early on he seemed to show more interest in girl-stuff, like playing with dolls and wearing dresses. We were cool with that; our attitude has always been to just stay out of his way and let him follow his own path. At the time, we thought, *OK, so our son is somewhat effeminate.*

But as he's grown older, Liko has become more boyish. He looks like a dude, and much of the time, he plays like a dude: trucks, space-ships, roughhousing, the whole knock-down, drag-out, fuck-shit-up package. He seems to have no problem at all relating to other boys.

But here's the funny thing: He never gave up the girl stuff. Left to his own devices, he still plays with dolls. Last week, he set up a daycare in our house, laying out little beds for each of his dolls and making sure that each one was fed, burped, changed, and napped. He likes ballet. He'll sit still for stories (something I've noticed girls are more likely to do) and he's always shown a lot of interest in other people's emotional states.

If boys are around, he plays the boy stuff; if surrounded by girlish girls, he plays princess. No problem. And he deals easily with kids who don't fit the gender binary: you might not be surprised to hear that the leader of his pack of boys at school is actually the most tomboyish girl I've ever seen.

The mixed dominance doesn't end there. He's multiracial and multicultural. His full name is Liko Wai-Kaniela Smith-Doo; that name is *almost* his cultural identity in a nutshell.

I say "almost," because the name doesn't account for the Judaism he's absorbed by attending a Jewish Community Center preschool for most of his life. One year, when we lit up our Christmas tree, he *covered his eyes* and whispered a Hebrew prayer. I'm not making this up. That's just the most amusing example of Liko's Jewish inclinations; he thinks of himself as Jewish (though we've explained that he was certainly not born that way) and many of his sensibilities and reactions are distinctively, instinctively Jewish.

I'll stop there; you get it, I'm sure.

It's easy enough to spot the aspects of his heritage and upbringing that might have produced this mixed dominance. Both parents participate in his care; we're a multiracial family; we sent him to the JCC (where my wife worked at the time); and so on. There are also idiosyncratic environmental factors. For example, all the rooms in our oddly shaped urban apartment are multipurpose—Liko's "room" is also our dining room and my work space (I'm typing there right now). I'm also looking out onto Castro St., where my son has grown up watching men holding hands and kissing.

Do I sound proud? In fact, I have wondered, many times, if we haven't screwed up our son. Will he get beaten up in junior high for being different? Will he be teased for having a funny name? Will he have trouble focusing, settling, specializing?

Those are the questions I ask in my darkest moments of doubt, often late at night when I ought to be sleeping.

But when I am well rested and high-functioning, as I am right now, I know what I really believe: that my mixed-dominant son is very well adapted for a cut-and-paste, twenty-first-century America.

We live in a mixed-dominance society—a multiracial, multicultural, multitasking, multigendered world of the future. We don't have jetpacks, but we do have a black president; cars don't fly, but women are now half the workforce; we haven't yet sent a human being to Mars, but this morning we watched a Serbian cat on a trampoline on YouTube.

Back in 2006, my entire family participated in a march for fair immigration laws. Afterwards, I pondered our family's mixed heritage. "We flutter together like quantum butterflies, every flap of our wings triggering hurricanes in times and places we can't even imagine," I wrote in my blog *Daddy Dialectic*.

> How did all these people, bedraggled and confused, traveling from every corner of the earth, come together to form Liko Wai-Kaniela Smith-Doo, my miracle, my hurricane? His name is a trainwreck; so's his bloodline. He's a mutt, my son, a walking, talking Amerieuroasiapacific mashup. I think he's pretty cool.

A relative of mine took offense to me calling my son "a mutt." She asked me to imagine Liko reading the entry as a teenager or young adult, how it would make him feel.

Actually, I have imagined that, many times. And I have a message for Liko in the future, should he happen to read this: Some people will try to make you feel different or wrong or odd for being who you are, kid. But your mother and I are proud of who you are—of who *we* are—and I hope you are able to see your mixed dominance as a strength. Find the other mutts in your world and build a community of mutts, where you help each other to eat with one hand and draw with the other, do the girl-stuff and do the boy-stuff, shield your eyes from the light of the Christmas tree.

In the twenty-first century, mutthood will be powerful!

Seeing Pink
Jason Sperber

Before my daughter was born, I knew what kind of father I wanted to be for her. My babygrrl was going to be raised to be a fierce, strong woman of color. I was going to make her iron-on onesies emblazoned with portraits of Yuri Kochiyama, Angela Davis, and Frida Kahlo. Her toybox would be filled with both dolls of color, preferably made by either anticorporate crafters or small indie companies, and things traditionally coded as "boy" like trucks and cars and tools. Both toy guns and Barbie would be equally verboten in our home, and her closet would be a pink-free zone. I knew the constricting, restricting and damaging messages the world would soon bombard her with about race and gender, and dammit if I wasn't going to all I could inside our home to inoculate her against them.

So yeah, it would've only served me right to have been gifted with a stereotypical "girly girl," a little karmic payback for putting all my crap on my poor baby's head before she was even born. That hasn't happened, luckily—while my Pumpkin's favorite color, for clothing and everything else, is, of course, pink, she does not, like her best friend since birth, demand to wear Disney Princess costumes as casual wear. As for my plans for a line of "Radical Mama" toddler-tees and stacking the deck toy-wise, well, the first toy I ever bought her was a "Little Frida" doll, and we dubbed the racially ambiguous doll we got her from a line of multiculti dolls by an alum of color from our alma mater, "Angela," because of her hair-do. bell hooks's children's books are on her overstuffed bookshelves. And because I'm not anticommercial per se but more anti–certain things (you know?), she's got more than her fair share of mass-produced goods featuring a certain brown-skinned Latina girl who likes to have adventures and help her animal friends, as well as her current favorite, the

Backyardigans (who, I'm convinced, are kids of color—I mean, Pablo? Tasha? Tyrone? Uniqua?)

Suffice it to say that as much as possible, her mother and I try to mediate potentially negative messages embedded in popular and commercial culture by controlling what she consumes (at least in our home) and by talking with her about things that might be problematic. But of course, none of this gets any easier as kids get older, with more and more outside influence impinging on them. During her year in day care, she'd come home talking about TV shows we didn't watch at home, or pretending to shoot things with her fingers like one of the little boys there. "Where did you learn that, Pumpkin?" we'd ask, before explaining why we didn't shoot things or people. Now that she's started preschool, I know there will be more of these teachable moments, even though we found as progressive and diverse a school environment as we could in our town.

But what's really got me thinking, about the subtle and insidious effect of both popular culture and the influence of other kids on how our Pumpkin learns to see the world and her place in it, is how she's started to label things as gender-appropriate or -inappropriate. It started cropping up during the recent holiday consumption season, during our trips to the local Target and Costco. One time, she was looking at some kids' room furnishings at Target, which, of course, are separated into a mostly blue boy aisle and a mostly pink girl aisle. There was some Thomas the Tank Engine stuff in the boy aisle, and she called out "Thomas!" happily when she saw it. "Want to look at that stuff, sweetie?" I asked. "No," she said, "that's for boys."

I stopped the cart. Say what now? She's always loved trains in general and Thomas specifically, so where did this come from? "No, love, anybody can play with Thomas, boys and girls, right?" But the moment was past and her attention was already on something else. But I was disturbed. I mean, I wasn't naïve, I knew these messages—what was appropriate for boys to play with, what was appropriate for girls to play with—were out there, bombarding her on TV and even in the choices and behaviors of her friends. But I always thought that the messages coming from home were enough to counteract these—that she could play with anything she wanted (well, not guns or Bratz, but you know what I mean), that she could do anything, that these things weren't limited because she was a girl.

Not long after, in the holiday gift section at Costco, I was checking out a Fisher Price kids' digital camera. There were two models, a big stack of blue toddler cameras and a big stack of pink ones. Apropos of nothing, The Pumpkin pointed at the two stacks: "That one's for boys and that one's for girls." "No, baby, anybody can have any color camera they want, right, Mommy? A boy can have a pink one and a girl can have a blue one if they want." But she wasn't having it; she knew who was supposed to have what, by color.

It was a digital camera, of all things. Of all the toys that did not need to be gender-coded, I thought, this would be it. It was the exact same toy, the only difference was the color. Did there really need to be a "boy" camera and a "girl" camera? I mean, c'mon! Needless to say, when it came time to buy presents, both the boy and the girls on our list got a different brand of camera—one that came in orange.

It doesn't end there. Where I always thought that I knew where the issues would be coming from—deflecting and deprogramming hegemonic lessons that toy kitchens were for girls and only boys could play with Tonka trucks from commercials that smacked of biological determinism—now even gender-neutral toys aren't so neutral. Does LeapFrog, for example, really need to make blue and pink versions of their kiddie learning computers? Is it that important to brand something as "for boys" or "for girls"? Will boys only use a computer if the learning game is branded with Disney's Cars? Will girls only use it if the game is branded with Disney's Princesses? And what if a girl likes Cars? Or a boy likes Princesses? What then? Or will they not even think to ask, having imbibed the blue=boy, pink=girl lesson for too long already?

I think about all the societal forces bombarding my daughter and her friends, and I don't want to feel powerless to do anything. The other night, one of The Pumpkin's best friends, a little boy she's known since birth, was frantic because he couldn't find another chair in which to sit at the kids' table for dinner. He refused, absolutely refused, to sit in a Dora-emblazoned chair because it was Dora, and Dora is for girls. No matter how much I or his parents tried to convince him that that wasn't the case, and that he could sit in the chair, he wouldn't change his mind. He wouldn't play dress-up with the girls, either, since the Disney Princess gear was obviously not for boys. Another boy in our group of friends, however, wouldn't hesitate to put on one of those tiaras. He unabashedly loves Dora and the Princesses, and his parents support that love. But what messages does he get at preschool, I wonder, from both teachers and other kids, when he shares that love with others?

I'm tired of seeing pink. I'm tired of seeing blue. And I'm both pissed off and saddened deeply that at age three, my daughter and her friends, both girls and boys, have already learned to see those colors, and what they are supposed to mean, so well. And I know that this isn't the last time I'm going to start a sentence with, "No, baby, both boys and girls can . . ."

Fighting the Market: Parenting and Gender
Simon Knapus

I was an established radical queer tranny vegan anarchist commie before I ever started trying to have kids, so I knew that somehow I would have to navigate for my child the space between our home and mainstream culture. Now the wide-eyed papa of a magical almost-three-year-old, I am beginning to realize what a firm grip the rest of the world has on our little universe. Preserving space for my kid's own identity to shine forth in all its glory is proving to be part of my everyday life in a way I never imagined back in those trying-to-conceive days.

I experience identity as a feeling of who I am. It is certainly ever-changing, but taken as a whole it grounds me to my experience of life, gives me continuity, and informs my actions—from everyday things like social interactions to trying to figure out what to do with my life. I think that identity requires the context in which it exists. If there were no "you," then there would be no need to define "me." As such, our identities must be influenced by what is going on around us, whether it be a worn-out dualistic gender scheme or the mega-corporations who pillage and plunder and hold nothing more sacred than money.

Gender and marketing are deeply linked because much of what we are told by advertisements (not just TV, but also licensed characters and brand names on t-shirts, toys, etc.) is that we need products to make us real (or at least better) men, women, boys, or girls. The message underlying all of this is that we are inadequate as we are, we are unhappy, we are not as manly or womanly or boyish or girlish as we should be, and we need things we never knew existed.

Mass marketing is rooted in psychology, in making us need things. Taking a cheap shot at identity is an easy way to get us to buy things because we want to feel secure in our identities. Furthermore, identity built up by mass marketing is much easier for corporate forces to manipulate. If I identify as someone who *loves* Elmo, then I will buy all the Elmo crap I can get my hands on. I will go into debt for it. I will buy it over other similar crap. Parents tend to want to make their kids feel awesome as much as possible, so if their kid *loves* Elmo then they will go for the easy smile and buy the Elmo crap. Grandparents, friends, aunts, uncles, housemates, will get Elmo for Junior when buying a gift because Junior *loves* Elmo. Elmo transitions to Dora and Spiderman and SpongeBob and the rest of the crew. The format is there: stuff to watch, wear, brush your teeth with, and so on. The change is merely in what stuff we are supposed to want at certain stages of our lives. The kids and their community are a well-trained consumer unit before the kids can poo on their own. Kids learn what it is to be a kid, a boy, a girl, a parent, a man, and a woman from the content of the product, but also from how it is sold. They are taught that it is extremely important to be a "real girl" or "real boy" and that "realness" is achieved through consumption.

One of the major successes of marketing is that it has created a dynamic with consumers where identity is more and more about what we buy than what we believe, who we love, where we live, or the other aspects of ourselves that can't be mass-produced but that shape our lives. I have no illusion about the role of clothing throughout history as having been a signal of class, ethnicity, sex/gender, age, occupation, etc., and thus reflecting and creating identity, but I think it is now more about what we buy than merely what we wear, and so much of what we buy advertises itself and other products and reinforces the systems that build and attack our identities.

For this reason, identity has become a major theme in my parenting approach. I want my kid to have room to interact with the world as a person who is guided by his own sense of right and wrong, his own desires for comfort and joy and growth and learning. I want him to express and explore his own identity without the burdens of a system that has a lot to gain by making him feel inadequate and then selling him stuff to give him a fleeting sense of joy or wholeness. I think he will enjoy life more and that he will have a more positive impact on the world this way. Perhaps I think so because it's been true for me. I completely concede that I am projecting my culture and values on my kid, but I guess in a way that's a necessary part of parenting.

I know that whatever I wear or whatever my son wears, people will assume things about us based on our clothing and appearance. I also know that we both really like to have fun with clothes and that we like being able to play and ready for anything. I am a single tranny/queer/genderqueer papa raising a kid with a penis. (There is a whole other discussion to be had about the decision to assign gendered pronouns to him based on his anatomy, which was a complicated one.) My son is not quite three yet, so I still have a big role in the decisions around what his clothing options will be, as well as what toys he has and what media he consumes and how he spends his time. Most of his clothes are traditionally masculine because that's more of what I am used to buying, and jeans or cords and a black t-shirt are easy to find at thrift shops. I choose to leave his curly hair long (because it's gorgeous) and dress him in a lot of pink, which seems to be more of an aberration for boys than it is for men. His hair gets in his eyes, so he wears barrettes, which he picks, which means they are generally pink and flowery. His favorite article of clothing is a red dress with a big pink kitty face. It seems that most of the world would have me say to him, "You can't have that because it's for girls." That bogus rigid gender system did me wrong, and I see no reason to push it on my kid just so that other people will be more comfortable. I have some skirts and fishnets tucked away for when I feel like wearing them, but my traditionally girly clothes don't make it into rotation nearly as often as his do. People respond to him differently when he is in "girl" clothes and also dresses and tights feel different on the body than "boy" clothes. I want him to have those experiences and I think they are valuable. Plus, he just loves to be fancy that way.

Another way I try to make space for my kid's identity, and the identities of others, is to help him interface with the world in a way that doesn't go first to gender. When talking about other people I say "person" not "man" or "woman" or "guy" or "lady." When talking about other children I say "child" instead of "boy" or "girl" (though I try to call kids people unless there are enough other people around that it would be confusing). First, those assumptions are often wrong. Second, I want him to think of people as people first and their sex or gender way on down the line.

I am a huge stickler about licensed characters. He doesn't watch, wear, or play with them. He's still young enough that I can pull this off, and I realize that it won't be the case forever. I think that they are simply clever marketing and I try to keep marketing out of his experience as much as possible, particularly marketing toward children. I think that it is stifling to his imagination, harmful to his self-image, tacky, harmful to the environment and other humans (sweatshops, plastics, etc.), and more. If he wants to advertise for mega-corporations like Disney when he is old enough to know what that means, he can of course, but part of my role as his parent is to navigate for him in matters he does not yet understand and to preserve his options for the future. I see allowing mega-corporations access to his mind, imagination, identity, desires, and billboard space harmful to his present and his future, and far more restrictive to him than my limits around licensed characters. That said, he has played with Spiderman characters at a friend's house and now can identify Spiderman pictures, etc. The conversation begins! I am very excited to teach him to be savvy about media and marketing, but I am also trying to do it on an as-needed basis until he is developmentally ready.

I want my kid to be free, to feel good about himself, to have a dynamic identity that is stable enough to guide him, but growing and flexible to change. I want him to find a gender approach that is fun and doesn't force him in to or out of things. I want for him to not have to experience the rollercoaster of inadequacy and temporary fulfillment that is set up to turn him into a mindless consumer. I want to figure out how to teach him to navigate the mainstream system without letting it limit him. It's hard work and I stumble a lot, but I'm trying.

Dads and Daughters, Fathers and Sons
Jeff West

My son Pip and my daughter Polly are the proud inheritors of my wife Ava's childhood collection of 1980s Cabbage Patch dolls, and last week they decided to take each doll in for a visit to the doctor. They do these visits periodically, designating one of the tables in our living room as an exam table and pulling out various utensils from the kitchen to serve as a stethoscope, an x-ray machine, etc. Pip usually takes the lead in this process, handing out roles to Polly and me and telling us what we should say at various points throughout the examination.

This time, Pip told me that I was to act as each doll's parent and that I should bring them into the examination room and explain to them what will happen during their visit with the doctor. He then handed me the first doll—a girl with stringy blond hair who we've named Olivia—and led us into the living room. As I walked in and sat down on the couch with Olivia on my knee, I was thinking ahead to naptime and how I needed to get a lasagna made for dinner, put a load of laundry in the wash, clean up the dishes from breakfast and lunch, and do some writing for the week's blog post during that time. After waiting in silence for a few seconds, Pip impatiently prompted me to start explaining to Olivia what he and Polly were going to do. Stuttering a bit to get my words out, I quickly said, "Um, Olivia, this is, um, Dr. Pip and Nurse Polly . . ."

Then I stopped, remembering as soon as the words had come out of my mouth that thirty-some years of enculturation create habits that are annoyingly hard to break. Without thinking, I had made my son the doctor and my daughter the nurse.

Polly and Pip looked over at me in confusion. I took a breath, paused for a moment, and then made a correction: "I'm sorry, Olivia, this is Dr. Pip and Dr. Polly."

· · · · ·

Taking care of Polly has brought me into direct and immediate contact with the mysterious world of women. While I thought I was ready for this, it turns out that, much like in rock climbing, there is a distinct difference between visualizing a route and executing the climb. From the ground it can be relatively easy to pick out the series of points one wants to hit, but up on the cliff, getting through those points is never that simple. With each move upward, new details emerge and new options appear, creating questions that challenge and complicate the previously established choices.

For example, dressing Pip each morning is relatively simple: I pull out of his drawer some variation of the same button-up shirt and khakis that I wear most days, throw on some athletic socks and tennis shoes, and run a brush through his hair. Polly's wardrobe choices require a whole other set of considerations: Is today a dress day or a pants day? Do I put bloomers on if she's wearing tights? Which pair of shoes is supposed to go with this outfit? How do I get these hair clips and hair bands in without her screaming in pain?

The questions take a more serious turn as intimations of sexuality appear: How short a dress am I willing to put on her? How low a top? Do I really want decals or words on the seat of her pants? What if they're just flowers? And why do some people insist on putting halter tops on two-year-olds? Do girls become sex objects the moment they can stand on their own two feet?

Even more seriously, Polly's presence in my life has made me hyperaware of how many historical inequalities of power between men and women are still present in our lives. At this writing, women in the United States earn an income that is only 80 percent of that received by men and only 15 percent of top-level managers are women. Of the 535 seats in the 112th edition of the United States Congress, only 93 are held by women. One in four women will become a victim of intimate partner violence in their lifetimes,

Every day I think about these statistics and contemplate what they mean for Polly's future. I wonder how I might prepare her to face these realities and what I might do to help her overcome some of the obstacles that create them.

My first instinct in this regard was to avoid making her excessively feminine. Driven by the idea that being "too girly" leads people to dismiss a woman or treat her as weak and incapable, I hypothesized that by keeping the pink to a minimum, avoiding the plague of Disney princesses and fairies, and cultivating interests in trucks, sports, construction equipment, Legos, electronics, and other "boy" topics, I could somehow make Polly immune to all the statistics. I imagined that as she grew up people would recognize that she was different, that she was better than all the other girls, and consequently they would not subject her to the same indignities that all the rest wind up suffering.

This hypothesis, of course, is ridiculous. Trying to essentially raise Polly as a boy is not the answer. For one thing, intentionally creating significant discord between what Polly understands about herself and what things are socially and culturally expected of her as a woman is unfair to her. This discord would only make things more difficult for Polly as she navigates through the world outside our door. For another achieving equality among men and women cannot be accomplished through the creation of sameness. Such attempts only instigate further oppressions by limiting everyone's life to the simplest and most linear of existences.

In the face of this false choice between Polly being too girly and not being girly enough, I have come to two conclusions. The first is that the best thing we can do right now for Polly is to create within our household small interventions in the dominant patterns of the world beyond. My hope is that through these interventions she will eventually become aware that the inequalities of power between women and men in our society are not natural and unalterable properties—and that this awareness will allow her to negotiate the inequalities she encounters with some sense of ironic separation between herself and her cultural position as a woman.

As such, I don't want to, for example, regularize the doctor=male, nurse=female equation in Pip and Polly's role-playing. This equation reproduces a relationship in which the highly paid man holds final decision-making power and the lower paid woman is responsible for following his directions. I'd rather have them enact the other possible combinations: Pip and Polly as doctors, Pip as nurse and Polly as doctor, Pip and Polly as nurses. She will see plenty of the first combination during her real visits to the doctor.

The other conclusion I have come to is that such interventions may not be as important for Polly as they are for Pip. As Ava has brought to my attention repeatedly, it's easy to think that addressing the patterns of gender inequality means altering how women operate in the world. But the reality is that the practices and habits of men drive the reproduction of these patterns. As beneficiaries of these inequalities, men bear greater power and responsibility for acknowledging and changing these patterns than is often recognized. For me living up to this responsibility means creating our interventions with Pip in mind as much as Polly. If Pip grows up sensitive to the historical practices of exclusion and obstruction that determine the unequal nature of the opportunities with which he and Polly are respectively presented in life, then perhaps he can further contribute to the type of cumulative cultural adjustment necessary to eliminate from our world the specter of the false choice and all the associated injustices that still haunt women today.

· · · · ·

After my slip that morning, I spent the next hour or so making a point of talking to Dr. Pip and Dr. Polly as I brought each of the dolls out for their turn in the examining room. Much to my relief, Pip eventually began parroting this manner of address as well. In some respects it seems like such a little thing, but at the moment these little things are what we can do. One day Ava and I will be able to have those conversations with Polly and Pip where we will talk about history and statistics and the reproduction of inequalities. For now, though, we have to try and show them what could be possible and hope that through this showing they learn to imagine and work for what the world should be instead of accepting as good enough what the world has already been.

You Skate like a Girl!
Jeremy Adam Smith

"Keep yer stick on the ice!" yelled a dad, his voice filled with anger.

"Come on, number fifteen!" yelled another. "You skate like a girl!"

Liko and I were watching a youth hockey game at the Yerba Buena rink in San Francisco. We were surrounded by fathers watching their boys play hockey . . . and, man, was it ugly.

As the kids battled on the ice, you could feel the tension rising among the parents.

Then I heard a lone, small voice from the other side of the bleachers:

"Have fun!" it said.

I looked up, and so did the other parents.

There stood a fellow on the top bleacher, smiling down at us. The smile said, C'mon, guys, lighten up.

I chuckled, and a ripple of laughter spread through the stands. We did lighten up.

One of the (few) moms yelled, "Have fun keeping your sticks on the ice!"

"Have fun skating like a girl!" shouted a dad.

Dads are way more active in sports than moms. In many communities, it's the main way that fathers play a role in the lives of their kids and other people's kids. Indeed, sports are the primary path many boys take to manhood.

That's both a good thing and a problem. It's a good thing because kids get exercise and they learn about discipline, focus, teamwork, and cooperation. It's a bad thing because in today's sports culture, they also learn about misogyny, homophobia, belligerence, self-destructive levels of competition . . . and the neuroses of their fathers.

"I've seen a lot of hardcore, winning-obsessed, hypercompetitive moms," says Regan McMahon, a friend and author of *Revolution in the Bleachers: How Parents Can Take Back Family Life in a World Gone Crazy over Youth Sports*. But fathers, says Regan, can be much worse. "It may be more common for men who have grown up playing sports to have certain opinions about how to be a star, or perhaps they want their child to have the success they had, or if they weren't a star, they want to experience vicariously the stardom they never achieved."

This leads to the kind of angry heckling I saw in the Yerba Buena bleachers; those guys are angry at their younger selves, first and foremost, and at the loss of their youth.

Inwardly, I was cringing: My son has been skating for two and a half years, and we were there so that he could participate in "Give-Hockey-a-Try Day" that afternoon. It's something he wanted, that I had resisted. The thought of my son entering this hockey culture, surrounded by these thuggish men, filled me with an old, sickening disquiet.

I'm not superior to these guys, and I know what Regan is talking about: I often find myself projecting my own athletic anxieties onto my son. I was a decent runner, but in team sports I was mediocre (soccer) to lousy (baseball). I very well remember the shit I got from both teammates and coaches, and I came to dread practices and games. By high school, I had stopped participating, and like millions of other freaks and geeks, I grew to hate sports and jocks. Today, when I see my son trying a sport, my stomach clenches as I watch for signs for failure and weakness.

That's not so different from the dads who stayed with sports, but never achieved as much as they hoped. While individual ability and commitment vary, the ultimate truth about sports is that, by definition, 99 percent of us won't become stars. The best we can hope for is fitness and fun, but too often our sports culture ruins our bodies through overtraining or ruins our self-esteem through bullying and hypercompetitiveness. That culture has shaped me as well as other fathers.

That afternoon, Liko suited up and skated out onto the ice, stick in hand. He was the smallest one on the ice, but I watched in awe, truly in awe, as he held his own. I watched him do his best, overcome obstacles, negotiate problems, recover from mistakes, take coaching, handle aggression from other kids, manage his own aggression, and gain new skills. All on his own.

Did this brave, strong boy really grow from the five-pound newborn who could fit in the palm of my hand? What a miracle. What a gift. I admit it: I was proud.

Again, that's a good thing and a bad thing, that pride.

"The father-son relationship is a delicate one, and boys really don't want to disappoint their dads," says Regan. "And I've seen many boys who seemed to care more about what their dad thought of their performance than their coach. One basketball star I knew would look up in the stands at his dad after every shot, not at his coach. I have heard, anecdotally, about a lot of kids—boys and girls—who want to quit a sport or a team but feel they can't because their dad doesn't want them too. That can strain marriages, too, when the dad is gung-ho and the mom isn't."

This might be the arena where dads can have the biggest impact in improving and repairing the world. I think about that dad who spoke up in the bleachers: "Have fun!"

It really made a difference, that small action; it took the emotion down a notch. Regan tells me that it's critical for dads to try to "be a voice of sanity in team meetings"—to emphasize the fun, to vote against yet another tournament or extra day of practice.

"Support your child's love of sports, but don't push them," advises Regan. "Keep your ego out of the equation. Keep in mind that your child is playing sports for his or her pleasure, not yours."

Jack and the Interstalk
Cory Doctorow

"Daddy, I want something on your laptop!" These are almost invariably the first words out my daughter Poesy's mouth when she gets up in the morning (generally at 5 a.m.). Being a life-long early riser, I have the morning shift. Being a parent in the twenty-first century, I worry about my toddler's screen time—and struggle with the temptation to let the TV or laptop be my babysitter while I get through my morning email. Being a writer, I yearn to share stories with my two-year-old.

I can't claim to have found the answer to all this, but I think we're evolving something that's really working for us—a mix of technology, storytelling, play and (admittedly) a little electronic babysitting that lets me get to at least *some* of my email before breakfast time.

Since Poe was tiny, she's climbed up on my lap and shared my laptop screen. We long ago ripped all her favorite DVDs (she went through a period at around sixteen months when she delighted in putting the DVDs shiny-side-down on the floor, standing on them, and skating around, sanding down the surface to a perfectly un-readable fog of microscratches). Twenty-some movies, the whole run of the Muppet Show, some BBC nature programs. They all fit on a 32 GB SD card and my wife and I both keep a set on our lap-tops for emergencies, such as in-flight meltdowns or the occasional restaurant scene.

I use a free, open-source video player called VLC, which plays practically every format ever invented. You can tell it to eliminate all its user interface, so that it's just a square of movable video, and the Gnome window-manager in Linux lets me set that window as "Always on top." I shrink it down to a postage stamp and slide it into the top right corner of my screen, and that's Poesy's bit of my laptop.

When she was littler, we'd do this for ten or twenty minutes every morning while she went from awake to awake-enough-to-play. Now that she's more active, she usually requests something—often something from YouTube (we also download her favorite YouTube clips to our laptops, using deturl.com), or she'll start feeding me keywords to search on, like "doggy and bunny" and we'll have a look at what comes up. It's nice sharing a screen with her. She points at things in her video she likes and asks me about them (pausable video is great for this!), or I notice stuff I want to point out to her. At the same time, she also looks at my screen—browser windows, email attachments, etc—and asks me about them, too.

But the fun comes when we incorporate all this into our storytelling play. It started with Jack and the Beanstalk. I told her the story one morning while we were on summer vacation. She loved the booming "Fee fi foe fum!" but she was puzzled by unfamiliar ideas like beanstalks, castles, harps and golden eggs. So I pulled up some images of them (using Flickr image search). Later, I found two or three different animated versions of Jack's story on YouTube, including the absolutely smashing Max Fleischer 1933 version. These really interested Poesy (especially the differences between all the adaptations), so one evening we made a Lego beanstalk and had an amazing time running around the house, play-acting Jack and the Beanstalk with various stuffed animals and such as characters. We made a golden egg out of wadded up aluminum foil, and a harp out of a coat hanger, tape and string, and chased up and down the stairs bellowing giant-noises at one another.

Then we went back to YouTube and watched more harps, made sure to look at the geese the next Saturday at Hackney City Farm, and now every time we serve something small and bean-like with a meal at home, there's inevitably a grabbing up of two or three of them and tossing them out the window while shouting, "Magic beans! Magic beans! You were supposed to sell the cow for money!" Great fun.

Every parent I know worries about the instantaneously mesmerizing nature of screens for kids, especially little kids. I've heard experts advise that kids be kept away from screens until the age of three or four, or even later, but that's not very realistic—at least not in our house, where the two adults do a substantial amount of work, socializing, and play from home on laptops or consoles.

But the laptop play we've stumbled on feels *right*. It's not passive, mesmerized, isolated TV watching. Instead, it's a shared experience that involves lots of imagination, physically running around the house (screeching with laughter, no less!), and mixing up story-worlds, the real world, and play. There's still times when the TV goes on because I need ten minutes to make the porridge and lay the table for breakfast, and I still stand in faint awe of the screen's capacity to hypnotize my toddler, but I wouldn't trade those howling, hilarious, raucous games that our network use inspires for anything.

How I Stopped Worrying and Learned to Love TV
David L. Hoyt

I t was a bitterly cold winter afternoon. Four p.m. and already dark. I was tired, and dreading the two-hour stretch that yawned before me, from the end of Spot's afternoon nap, to Spot's mom coming home from work a little after six.

It is a bleak stretch of time, bleak in my mind like the glare of sodium vapor street lamps over a frozen, salt-crusted alley.

I looked down at my hand. It held the remote. I looked at the TV. It was dark. I thought about my options.

Option A: *Don't turn on the TV*. I knew what was in store without it. Some time in the kitchen, sitting at the counter and moving the cereal boxes around; maybe I would do some dishes. Then some time on the couch, reading that week's favorite clutch of books five times. Then maybe I'd do a few loads of laundry. Then perhaps back to the kitchen to supervise the unpacking of all the drawers and the arrangement of their contents on the dining room table, punctuated with occasional collapses onto the floor in a hysterical fit of tears.

For two years, we banned the TV, and I made no use of the babysitter's best friend. Instead, I *was* the TV. I took Spot on walks when the weather was nice. We went to the park, to the art center, to the cafe. We stayed inside and read when it was cold, and we played with blocks and pegs and balls and boats. We wrestled, chowed down, and stacked a whole lot of stuff.

Sometimes, when I was just too tired or sick, I would simply lie down and sleep while Spot clambered over me. But I never turned on the TV.

Until the other day, after the two year moratorium expired, and I chose . . .

Option B: *Turn on the TV*. I raised the remote and hit the "on" button. Without a word, summoned like a zombie to a shopping mall full of screaming people, Spot calmly crawled up onto the couch and sat under my arm, all agitation drained from his limbs, his eyes wide and his heart slowed. He sat in a perfect "L" position, legs straight out in front of him on the flabby sofa, hands at his sides, giant floppy fleece slippers outlined against the blue glow of the TV screen. Spot hadn't been beside me this still, this close, for this long since he was a newborn.

For no particular reason, on came *The Manchurian Candidate*, followed by an episode of *Star Trek: The Next Generation*. There are some violent scenes in *The Manchurian Candidate*—a movie, coincidentally, about hypnosis—and I was too slow with the remote to prevent Spot from seeing the scene where one dude takes a pistol and blows the head off another dude.

Whoops! That was bad!

But nothing happened. No crying, no physical jolt, no worried look up to Dad for reassurance. I don't think Spot can tell the difference between a man getting his head blown with off with a revolver and Barney getting hit in the head with a soccer ball. But Spot can tell you if there's a BALL involved.

Spot engages with television on an extremely concrete basis. Of the many levels of narrative meaning that criss-cross and overlap in any movie or TV show, Spot is most interested in the level of the Household Noun.

Pay no attention to the photon torpedoes, to Worf's head, to Riker's beer gut, or any of the funky aliens. What Spot will share his appreciation for are all the BALLS that come out of nowhere. There are also lots of STARS, maybe a MOON or two, some NIGHT, and the people wearing HATS which are sometimes hard to tell from their HEADS. There are also sometimes PURPLE PEOPLE.

There are also many things that don't appear in *Star Trek*, but Spot points these out too, because it is not their fault that these things have been excluded from *Star Trek*. Among them are PUPPIES, BARNS, and BEARS. Neither were POTTY, PEE-PEE, and BULB identifiable, and there seem to be no STAIRS on the Starship Enterprise.

So that was the end of our two-year moratorium on TV. Some gratuitous violence, some cheesy yet oddly uplifting syndicated sci-fi, and about two thirds of the way through it Spot turns over and starts pointing at the parts of my face. Glasses, nose, ears.

"Spot, Picard just ordered a saucer separation. Dude, you NEVER see this . . . it's very rare. Chill out for a sec."

So Spot does me a favor and sticks around for the saucer separation, which oddly enough gives me chills, and then mom comes up the stairs like she does every night. Time's up! My household hobbit swings his slippered feet off the couch. Whatever Spot thought of what we were watching, clearly he thought it had gone on too long. It was time to show mom the various projects he had left in different stages of completion.

Sinking ever deeper into the flabby sofa cushion, I took a deep breath, and changed the channel.

The Force of "The Force"
Craig Elliott

I introduced Star Wars to my son last year when he turned seven. The movies had a huge influence on me as a kid, and I am still a big Star Wars geek. Admittedly, I was excited at sharing this with my kids when they were old enough.

The opening scene of the movie was just as amazing and awe-inspiring as I remembered it in 1977: the scrolling titles, the wonderful score, and the ship flying in from the top of the screen, all of which sucked me in. It was truly magic. I was eight when my parents took me and it changed my world. I was overcome with joy to see my son's eyes wide open, become thrilled with the adventure about to unfold, and snuggle up to me on the couch. It was a magical fathering moment for me, and one that reflected that magic I felt those many years ago in the theater. And as was the case with me, the movie spurred my son's imagination, and inspired a new level of inquisition: reading, dreaming, and asking questions on how our world works. He began to immerse himself in Star Wars, reading, and playing, and drawing. I was pleased that he loved something that I loved and it was exactly what happened to me.

All in all, it went well. But what started out as innocuous imagination building has, in the last year, become a steady array of violence. Both kids—now the youngest one still hasn't actually watched any of the movies or cartoons but knows the whole lore from his friends and big brother—take great fun running around the house with their light sabers slicing up the dog, the cats, each other, the furniture; or wield their imaginary guns shooting up the house and "killing" countless "bad" people.

What happened? What happened to my Star Wars movies in my house? What happened to my sweet, loving, and innocent kids? I don't remember responding like this in my youth, and it seems to me that the marketing of Star Wars these days is focused more on the wars, the aggression, and death. Sadly, Star Wars reflects the dark, violent times in our daily reality. I wasn't prepared for this result, and as a peaceful, feminist father who has worked hard to counter the aggression in my own life, it hurt to see my kids replicating the violence in the bigger world.

My partner, Nicole, and I have raised our two boys with intention toward love and graciousness, kindness, and care. We have encouraged them to love instead of hurt, and to play with sweetness, compassion, and thoughtfulness. We have also shared with them some of the inequities that are played out on the schoolyards, our cities and our country, and asked them to challenge them in their own little ways. With all this Jedi-killing in our house, I felt a bit like a fraud.

It is a reminder for me how ever-present the violence and war metaphors are in our daily, modern lives. I felt like the fraud not because my kids were acting against their nonviolent upbringing, but because I had allowed the violence to break our "bubble" of the home. It was destined to happen at some point anyway, but I had been hoping, perhaps naïvely, to protect them from the "dark side" of our world just a bit longer. It is a sharp reminder of how our consciousness and action needs to match the developmental processes our kids are taking. As their worlds expand, so must our socially conscious parenting, so that we match their bigger world with our bigger actions and values of peace, justice, and love.

We practice our socially conscious parenting through ongoing dialogue with our children about the actions and behaviors of the characters they encounter, in worlds both imagined and physical, centering on love, compassion, cooperation, and peace. We also bring intention to our parenting roles so that we demonstrate as much as we can how to live these values in a complex world that does not always share them. When we stumble, that same intention allows us humility to acknowledge that we did not "do what we said" and commit to doing better. In this case, I discussed with my son that hope, love, and harmony were equally powerful forces to aggression, fighting, and death. Even a young Jedi can understand love in the midst of fighting if enough of it is around for him or her to experience.

In this galaxy, not-so-far-away, I have hope that a new way of living is possible, with love and caring rather than fighting and violence. I have hope that this "new" reality mirrors the original essence of the movie rather than the other way around. I have hope that the force of love is more powerful.

I'll let you know how it goes.

Boys, Toys, and Militarism
Chip Gagnon

It's hardly controversial to argue that war and instruments of killing are glorified in our society, and that young boys are a particular target of this promotion.

Just walk down the "boys" aisle of any toy store and you see that a huge proportion of toys are military-themed or military-related. My local dollar store, in fact, in its toy section, carries nothing but military toys for boys. Some video games also promote the sense that warfare is fun.

And I do believe there is a connection between this promotion of military toys and the tendency of many Americans, especially men, to cheer and support U.S. military action abroad without thinking about the costs to those on the receiving end of U.S. military action, without thinking of the costs to the U.S. soldiers who take part, without thinking about what war really is.

When my son BK was born, we began facing the question of how we wanted to raise him, what kind of man did we want him to become. Part of the concern was the hypermilitaristic boy culture in our society, which was reinforced by the typical macho stereotypes foisted on boys from a very very early age.

But then we started to see that our son liked to shoot at things, even though he had no toy guns, even though he did not watch television or violent movies. He found a stick and would use it as a gun. We were quite concerned about this kind of thing.

One day I ran into the son of friends of ours who was about twenty. His parents had been active in the peace and feminist movements from the time he as born. He himself is a very cool kid, not at all militaristic or macho. In fact, I'd be thrilled if my own son turned out like this kid.

I talked to him about my concerns—BK was probably about five years old at the time. And he told me his own story. He'd grown up in a feminist, peace-activist household. Yet he loved to play army and war, he loved to play violent video games. It seemed like such a contradiction.

But he explained that he knew the difference between fantasy and reality. Because his parents had actually talked to him about war, warfare, killing, and militarism, he understood that the fantasies of playing army or playing violent video games were very different than actual warfare.

And as I thought about it, I realized that as a kid I also played army. We'd divide up into opposing armies, and roam the neighborhood "killing" each other with pretend guns. Although there were no video games back then, we watched plenty of TV shows and movies that glorified military action.

And yet, I did not become a militaristic, violent guy.

The point here is that the attitudes of our kids come from many different places. Yeah, there's a lot of pressure and opportunity for our boys to adopt a militaristic mindset, to think of war as "cool" and of violence as normal.

But we parents are our kids' first teachers. Given this societal environment, it's so important that we actually talk to our sons about militarism and war. Of course we need to talk to our daughters about it. But our sons are the main targets, and when they turn eighteen, the sons of those of us in the U.S. are required to sign up for "selective service" (military service registry).

Given U.S. foreign policy over the past several years—actually, over the past half-century—and given the extent to which U.S. military action is glorified in the news, in history books, in newspapers, it's especially important for us as Americans to talk openly and frankly with our kids, and especially our sons, about militarism.

My wife and I have done that. From the time he was little, we made sure BK knew what war actually was, putting it in very human terms. We explained the difference between doing something to defend yourself, and doing something that is closer to bullying. We explained what fighting a war means for people on the receiving end of our missiles and bullets—not just soldiers but moms and dads and kids. We explained exactly what happens in a war—people actually get killed and maimed, homes are destroyed—conveying the immense sadness and tragedy that comes with violence. We explained that unfortunately sometimes leaders, including our own, do not obey the most basic rules of nursery school—use words, not your hands.

All of this helps make it clear that playing war and "shooting" with sticks, pushing buttons on a GameCube or watching a DVD are not war. They are fantasy. And war is fundamentally different.

Our kids have to know that war is not a game, and that violence should only be used as a very last resort. They have to know that our society tries to create the false impression that war is exciting and fun and bloodless. They have to know that our leaders try to deceive us into believing that we are always justified to use bombs and guns.

Of course BK has a lot of nonviolent toys, and he and his friends do a lot of other kinds of play that does not involve war or guns. But when BK plays army, when he plays with his plastic army guys, when he and his friends—including a good friend whose parents are feminist and pacifist and pretty much on the same page as we are on those issues—have gunfights, with sticks, with Super Soakers, with toy guns (yes, BK somehow has a toy revolver, the kind I had as a kid, and his friends do too), he understands that this is not war. BK plays with the toys, but he understands that the reality of war is not a game.

Section Three

TWEENS AND TEENS

Low and Slow:
A Movie Script about a Father, Three Kids,
the Evil Media, and the Perils of Sex Education
Tomas Moniz

Voiceover (imagine the baritone of Morgan Freeman): I always thought this would be easy. I humored myself with assurances that I wouldn't handle the subject like my parents did, that I would be a beacon, a guide, dare I say a confidante for my children.

Ah, the bullshit we tell ourselves when we're rocking babies about how we will parent in the future. Let me tell you right off what the moral of this story will be: humility.

Scene 1: I'm driving in my car with my thirteen-year-old son; I discovered a few days earlier he's acquired some pornographic material. I know what you're thinking. What's the big deal about some adult magazines tucked up under a mattress. Oh, how I long for those good ol' days. You see, if only I discovered a dirty magazine. Nooooo. Thanks to the Internet, instead I discovered forty-five-second clips of hardcore group sex on my computer desktop.

It's time for *The Talk,* which I've had many times before, so this should be easy. Hey, I found some . . . stuff . . . on my computer I think we need to talk about.

Awkward silence.

Really? What? he asks.

More awkward silence.

He continues, do we have to talk about it?

Cue cheesy music.

As I pull over, I mumble something like, well, if you're gonna look at it, I guess we need to talk about it

I'll spare you the gory discomfort but let me tell you, joking about sex with him when he was ten was nothing like having the first real conversation with him at thirteen about the seriousness and the responsibilities of sexuality.

Flashback: I'm standing with my father in the garage. It's dusk. I'm about fourteen or fifteen. I rarely have time with him alone anymore because he's a busy man, he's a silent man, but I know he loves me, I know he tries. He doesn't look me in the eyes. He called me out here because he caught me the other night getting down like only teenagers can in the horrifically uncomfortable backseat of my '76 Toyota Corolla.

So now comes my *The Talk.*

Listen, he tells me, and waits, the pause pregnant with anticipation.

He says, keep your willy in your pants. I'm serious. Then he walks away. And I'm serious; that's what he said, the extent of our birds and bees conversation.

Of course, soon his advice becomes my way of joking with my girlfriend about getting it on, it's time to release the willy; it was funny until at the age of eighteen she becomes pregnant.

Non Sequitur Flash Forward: the horror and accompanying popcorn gag as my son and I were getting ready to watch *Aladdin* (don't ask why my son was invited to a three-year-old's birthday party at a movie theater) when I witness for the first time the preview for the movie *Free Willy.*

Scene 2: After having a difficult discussion about drug use with my fourteen-year-old daughter, I jokingly ask her, well anything else we should talk about, like are you having sex?

Now, of course, I joked with her too from around age four about sex, but once again I'm not really prepared for her response.

No, dad, I mean I've made out with a few hot boys that's all.

I stare blankly at her.

And, once again, in a moment that highlights the generational differences between my teenage years when you had to have a girl/boyfriend to free willy, today's young people are more empowered to be sexually active without having to have a significant other; the wisdom is shocking.

I stutter something like, I didn't even know you had a boyfriend . . .

I don't.

Oh?

Picking up on my mental conundrum, she explains, there are boys you want to be your boyfriend and then there are hot boys you just wanna kiss.

Still stuck somewhere in the 1950s, I ask, but don't you want your boyfriend to be hot?

Yes, but sometimes you just want to kiss a hot boy. Can you leave my room now?

Voiceover: The third time really is the charm. I understand that now. From the sheer horror at the need to talk with my son about masturbation and pornography, to the disorientation of generational changes with my middle child, to finally the self-reflection, the epiphany of, Oh, I've been here before with my youngest. Now some people may not need three children to see the light; unfortunately, I did. Of course, my cynicism almost makes me blow it again. And here's where I blame the evil media. I hate all this faux female bisexuality (it's almost never male) that has become a pop culture trend; it's all over YouTube videos, hip-hop songs, and Facebook groups.

Scene 3: When my youngest daughter informs me that she's joining the Gay-Straight Alliance at her middle school, I almost miss it. When I was twelve, I was still playing with tractors and thought my willy was indeed a whale.

Uh huh, I mumble while trying to decide what the hell to make for dinner for two daughters who never want the same thing.

But after a second, her words reach me. I remember my father, the dark garage, the silences. I stop what I am doing, and I look at her. I tell her how proud I am of her. I ask her questions, and I just listen.

And a few weeks later, I listen again as she shares with me her frustration that even people who are members of the alliance use the word gay derogatorily.

And later still, I apologize to her when she overhears me joking with a neighbor about a friend of ours who is a self-proclaimed *fag hag.* I see her face; I know immediately she only hears me saying the word fag.

Scene 4: We are watching the movie *La Mission*; it's three teenage girls and me. At first they wanted to see *Hot Tub Time Machine*. To be honest, I did as well, but I knew that it's not often we get to see movies that bring up issues critically. It's true though that even bad movies are opportunities to discuss the way things are fucked up: sexual violence, gender rigidity, racism; but tonight I wanted to go the high road. We're in the dark, and it's the scene in which the father is refusing to listen, to know about, to acknowledge his gay son's desires. It's the familial version of "don't ask, don't tell." We're in the dark, and my daughter reaches to grab my hand; she leans into me and says, I can't believe there are still people like him.

It's then that I am thankful for the privilege of being a part of communities in which the homophobia I remember as a teenager seems surreal, seems like Hollywood exaggeration to my teenage daughters.

Voiceover: I rented *The Times of Harvey Milk* and planned on watching it with my kids, but now they're busy, now they have so many other things to do that they just wanted to watch the funny parts. Funny? you might ask. They simply love the scenes of street life in the Castro. They comment on the clothes, the hairdos, laugh at the Castro street parade footage, the dancing. But as the story shifts to the spontaneous memorial that moved down Market Street after Harvey Milk was killed, they watch silently; I see their sadness, feel their disbelief. They soon leave and return to their rooms. I don't have to say anything. They know.

And when I tell them about the event I'll be reading at a few weeks later to celebrate San Francisco's first annual Harvey Milk Day, they smile and one adds, that's cool, but just don't embarrass me, OK?

So it's come to this. Even though I don't have to explain things anymore and even though I am so clearly the last person they want to confide in about anything sexual, I still ask questions. And they still hate it.

I still ask if they are *having drugs and doing sex*. They just roll their eyes and look utterly offended. My mantra now to them is *low and slow*; I've stolen the line from *La Mission*. I tell them in my best vato accent to have fun but keep it *low and slow*.

I think it's better than telling them about willies and freedom.

Radio Wars
Zappa Montag

Music is pretty much my religion. Given my roots, I almost had no choice but to be a follower of the Church of Music. I was born to young, hippie parents in 1969, and named after a rocker who was decidedly unpop. My mom is a black New Yorker, who can probably name every garage band that made the scene in the '60s or '70s. My father is a Hungarian Jew who came to New York City when he was seven. He thought of himself as an honorary brotha for a while, and he loved Ray Charles, Sam Cooke, Hank Williams Sr., Bob Marley, and the Stones.

He was the one who mostly raised me in our redwood forest home in Northern Cali, and it's from him I inherited my philosophical, exploratory, laid-back fathering style. Like my dad, I have an underlying belief in my children's intelligence, adaptability, and ultimate right to self-determination. I try to teach and demonstrate open-mindedness and a live-and-let-live approach to life. But now as my daughter becomes a teen, I am starting to wonder if I am the dad I want to be. Her clothing style doesn't faze me. I am not a girl, never was, so who I am to decide what a twelve-year-old girl should wear (as long as it isn't hoochified, or more expensive than our meager budget affords)? When she decided to go Goth, I had no problem. I grew up with hippies, punkers, and other social-boundary pushers. It would bother me more if she didn't have a rebellious streak.

Nope, the things that gets me is her love of the pop culture that seems to be so perfectly marketed to ensnare the minds of cool kids like her, and turn them into mindless drones of consumerism and shallow vanity. This is especially irksome when it comes to her taste in music, and when I hear the radio in her room constantly tuned to a tweeny bopper station playing the latest whiny noise from Katy Perry, I want to burst in and demand she put on some Sam Cooke. Everybody watches crappy TV and dumb movies, but music is different to me. Either you have good taste in music (like me, naturally), or you are a culturally deficient loser. At least that is how I see it. And I don't want to be responsible for raising one of those types.

So when we are getting in the car and I hear her say "Daddy . . ." I already know what's coming, and I snap, "*No!*" before she finishes her sentence. "No what?" she asks. "No, you can't choose the radio station!" I growl. This radio battle is ground zero in my struggle to impart the necessary tools of coolness to my dear child before she enters the world of teenage wackiness—and ultimately becomes a creature who is beyond my sphere of influence. The car is my realm, and I rule the car radio. Oldies rock and soul stations are the soundtrack to my travels. Not black music, or white music, just plain good music. At least that is how I have chosen to see things. And despite my laid-back intentions and commitment to free expression, I admit it: I use the car radio to indoctrinate my kids.

Thankfully I can say that I have achieved some success. My daughter does at least love some Sam Cooke and has begun to understand that the cool songs from the *Shrek* soundtrack were actually in existence way before the giant, green monster ever showed up in a theater near you. She listens to the combo of rock, soul, and funk tunes that come from my stations and knows many of the songs by heart as well as I do. So she doesn't get "Stairway to Heaven" and she hates reggae. There is plenty of time to work on that. At least she knows who Aretha Franklin is. And occasionally, every once in awhile, when I am feeling nice or don't feel like fighting with her, I put on one of her tween stations and let her teach me all about the ways of "the Bieber" and his ilk. And you know what? Justin Bieber is not as bad as I would have thought.

Skate Dad
Mark Whiteley

As a thirty-four-year-old skateboarder who has had the good fortune of keeping a close group of friends for the better part of two decades, I've seen a lot of different eras and transitions in the lives of these young-turned-middle-aged men. The rites of passage I've been witness to span from first getting a driver's license to first paying a mortgage, and as many of my compatriots enter the era of the latter, many of them have begun bringing offspring into the world. As more and more dudes become dads, I'm noticing a remarkable statistic rising in tandem: A good 75 percent of my skater friends have fathered girls. Coincidental rolls of the genetic dice, or karmic revenge for years of objectification, one-night stands, and serial assholery? You decide.

Let's first look back at some factors that may have contributed to many skateboarders of my generation mishandling (ahem) their relationships with girls and women during their younger days. Foremost is the cold, hard fact that skateboarding is really hard. To improve and be good at it, which is every skater's goal, requires so much dedication and time spent doing it that it doesn't leave room for much else in your life if you are really focused on it, which most skaters are. This instantly limits your exposure to girls on a temporal basis alone—there's no way you are going to learn 360 flips if you are following girls around the mall in your spare time. In the '80s and '90s, skateboarding became increasingly technical, with new and more difficult tricks springing up constantly, and if you weren't keeping up or you were doing them poorly, you were definitely going to be endlessly ridiculed by your friends. Therefore, you skated a lot, which meant in the almost exclusively boys-club demographic, you spent very little time around girls.

In fact, at around sixteen when my friends and I decided that maybe we wanted to spend some time trying to be around girls instead of trying 360 flips all night, we had such little experience that we didn't even know where to start. We decided to go down to the local teen hangout, a Tower Records, and look for girls. It didn't go well. The girls either laughed and ran off when we approached them or wouldn't even acknowledge us. We got frustrated and gave up quickly, and once again lured by the siren's call, went off into the corner of the parking lot to practice our 360 flips. Strangely, we had better luck when we forgot about trying to talk to girls and were just off in our four-wheeled world. A car full of young ladies we had never seen before appeared out of nowhere and came screeching by us, one of them stretching out the back window to raise her shirt and flash us while giddily yelling, "Woooooooo!" That first image of glorious, real live breasts was burned instantaneously into my brain, no matter that they had been traveling away from me at twenty miles an hour and at distance of a dozen yards. Of course, when en masse we tried to chase them down, it was, "Later, skaters!" and a puff of exhaust to the face.

Socially, skaters of my generation were not blessed with the cool cachet that following generations were granted by television programs and pop culture references along the lines of "Sk8er Boi." We were hated by the jocks, disregarded by the cool kids, not smart enough for the smart kids, and then the theater geeks and D&D weirdos weren't cool enough for us. This, too, cut off many of our options for exposure to girls. Only the goth and punk girls liked us, but they always had goth and punk boyfriends already. In the early '90s, hip-hop and graffiti culture became more intertwined with skating, and the population of that new world was cool and acceptant of us, but the girls there also already had boyfriends, many of whom were much tougher than we were. So, all that said, high-school-age skaters of my generation just didn't have many girls around. We were basically nerds, just not in the academic sense. Enter porn.

Well, sort of. In the pre-Internet days we were still too young to legally get the real thing, but we took what we could get—sometimes from older brothers, sometimes lifted out of that same Tower Records, sometimes in the form of those Victoria's Secret catalogs that came to our moms in the mail, and strangely, sometimes on our skateboards themselves. Apparently, even many of the professional skaters of the day were suffering from the same lack of female companionship as we were (or equally likely, the companies making the boards recognized our state of affairs and knew they could capitalize on it). The early '90s saw a rash of skateboards featuring graphics of women. Some of the more iconic ones were of then-current supermodels such as Claudia Schiffer and Cindy Crawford, while others went a little further with greatly detailed illustrations of naked women, photos of women in bikinis which were actually stickers that could be removed to reveal the subjects beneath, and even one board featuring a point-of-view photo of a guy looking down at a slightly obscured pile of porn mags and a bottle of lotion, his bare legs visible from the knees down. In retrospect it is not clear to me why this was an image a guy would want on his board—essentially advertising the fact that he was a chronic masturbator with no girlfriend—but at the time it was a pretty sought-after board.

As time went by and we entered our late teens and early twenties, inevitably we started to do better. Girls got more adventurous, and alcohol probably helped. I lucked out and landed a long-term girlfriend, but still had a front row seat for many of the wonderful, laughable, terrible interactions my friends were to design and implement over the following years. As horny young men with newfound access but without a ton of experience around female companions, many of them tended to go for the gusto a little too quickly and either scare off or offend their intended love interests/targets. When luck was with them and things did go well at that point, it often ended badly sooner than later because when the girls would want to spend more time together, it was, "Sorry, I'm going skating." For most skaters at this age, no girl is going to take the place of skating, and knowing that once a girl discovers that fact they will be gone, many skaters start working with the mindset of "get the girl to put out as much as you can right now because there is no later." And thus is born a horrible modus operandi for dealing with girls, and what's often created is a serial asshole who goes from girl to girl to girl, breaking hearts along the way. Anybody who remembers the movie *Kids* knows the extreme this behavior can go to. Now, imagine this scenario on repeat for years on end, from house party to house party, and you can just see the bad karma getting thicker and thicker.

Fast forward ten years or so, and most skaters have matured, realized there is more to life than skating, gained some other experience, spent some time with women, and generally settled down. This is the case with many of my friends, many of whom are now married or in long-term relationships, and more and more of whom are starting to have kids. Strangely the vast majority of skaters I know with kids have had daughters, and many have had multiple daughters—myself included. Obviously chromosomes are the real decision makers in that department, but part of me believes that this, in at least some instances (not my own, as I am a decent and upstanding gentleman), is karmic payback for past trespasses and offenses against girls, and now the skater dads must look forwards to and eventually deal with their own daughters dating idiots just like themselves.

But in many ways, this will make them better fathers to their own daughters as they will know first-hand what to look out for, and they will be able to see it coming from a mile away. Skaters know almost everything there is to know about drugs, drinking, ditching school, sneaking out, and general hooliganism; they know how to talk their way out of things with cops if trouble arises; and if there is one thing skaters are experts at, it is the art of vibing. I have never seen another group of people so adept at making others feel totally unwelcome, uncool, and self-conscious with hardly speaking a word, or maybe a few very choice underhanded ones. Skaters often implement this harsh psychological hazing system to protect their group or territory from unwanted or undeserving trespassers. Transfer that treatment to when a skater's daughter brings a guy home—that guy is in for a seriously uncomfortable meeting-the-parents experience, several times over, until he proves himself in a big way. If a skater is accustomed to using such psychologically damaging tactics to protect a cement ledge against a group of people just like himself, imagine how that will be amplified and inflicted when focused on somebody who's object of desire is the skater's daughter. I know that in about ten years, my deep-rooted and well-practiced vibing skills will be in regular and heavy use, and I will be glad to have them. I pity the fool who brings my daughters home late.

But on the brighter side, I see a lot of my friends becoming wonderful fathers to their daughters for much more positive reasons. The culture of my generation's skateboarding world was one that brewed up a stew of creative, artistic, musical, playful, ethnically diverse and racially tolerant guys who have a strong sense of community, a DIY ethic, love to travel, are hands-on, and are open to new ideas and different ways of doing things. As we inevitably transfer some of these interests and traits to our daughters, we encourage nontraditional activities, behavior and thought processes that defy long-standing norms for bringing up girls. Physically, skaters get very used to trying something over and over until it works, so we have a lot of patience and determination when trying something new and can pick ourselves up from a fall with no trouble. I find myself holding my daughters to these standards as they become more physically active. "Want to swing across the monkey bars? Give it a try, don't be scared! Your hands slipped and you fell? Dust yourself off, let's get back up there. One bar at a time, we'll get it." No coddling. They know you can't be scared to try, and if it doesn't work right away, you just get up and try again, without hesitation. Artistically, we *want* our kids to color outside of the lines. A lot of the time when I draw with my kids, we'll play a game called Squiggle—I make a random line, they turn it into something else. Look at it from this side, from that side, it is positive space or negative space? Could that curve in the line be a nose, a mountain, a bumper? Skaters look at objects in their surroundings and see the potential for what they could be used for, and Squiggle is a prime example of taking that way of looking at what's in front of you and applying it for other purposes. And then in terms of community, the skateboard population has such a diverse makeup that we end up exposing our kids to quite an array of people and ways of life. In my group of skate friends I have tar moppers, teachers, architects, firemen, artists, accountants, musicians, guys who live in mansions, guys who have no home, straight guys, homosexual guys, guys from all ethnic backgrounds, and my girls have been exposed to all of them and accept them all the same. Skateboarding is wonderful in that it can unite people from extremely divergent walks of life, people who would otherwise have nothing in common, and expose them to each other and help them learn about people and the world in a way that many "teenage" activities can't touch. These are all things that will make us into good role models and benefit our girls as they grow up to be the interesting, fun-loving, and well-rounded young ladies we hope they will become.

Just don't even think about trying to date them.

Mad Dad
Chip Gagnon

Sadly, some of my most vivid childhood memories are of my dad getting really angry at me and my brother. I know he wasn't mad all the time, and I do have other memories of him as well. But the times he got mad at us stay with me even after all these years. My dad came from a long line of mad dads. His own dad hit his sons with a belt, and there's the story of how he threw one of his sons into a snow-bank. His dad's dad was apparently an abusive alcoholic whose kids left home as soon as they could. At least my dad didn't drink, but his emotions often seemed to be limited to the range between annoyance and anger.

From the time my daughter was born sixteen years ago, I promised myself that I'd be a different kind of dad. I stayed at home full time with my daughter for her first two years. I never once hit or spanked my daughter or her younger brother. Though I yelled occasionally, overall I tried to be understanding and loving. I cuddled and hugged them a lot. I explained to them my expectations of them, why I had those expectations, and the consequences of not doing the right thing. I cultivated their abilities to make their own choices. I spent a lot of time with them as they were growing up. And I thought I was doing a great job.

But recently my daughter has accused me of being mad all the time. And she might just be right. I don't know why or how, but I've gotten into a pattern of being angry with her a lot. How could that be?

I think back to when it started. It was when she was in seventh grade or so. She began to get that teen attitude that just drove me crazy. She'd pick fights with us over small things. She'd give us those teen looks. Yeah, I knew it was a phase that teens go through. And overall she was a good kid, no major problems. But she was kind of pushing us away, and pushing our buttons.

But on the other hand, I still had long talks with her, we'd go on walks, we'd do things together. So there was this back and forth between conflict and getting along. But then in ninth grade she really started pushing away. She still talked to us, did things with us. And she wasn't getting into major trouble; I don't want to exaggerate this. But on the other hand, she was going her own way, and acting in ways that made me feel like a failure as a parent.

Okay, she's sixteen. It's been really hard for me to emotionally understand that she's almost an adult now, that she's not my little kid anymore. I mean, rationally of course I know that. But emotionally I think I wasn't sure how to deal with it. It was hard, and what I'm realizing is that my range of emotional abilities is more limited than I'd thought: another victim of guy culture, despite the feminist consciousness.

My daughter is highly verbal, articulate, and has a very keen eye for analyzing social situations. I find talking to her to be exhausting when we're on topics of how we treat her, how "strict" we are, how awful life is in our small town, how she can't wait to get out into the big wide world. She seems able to turn everything around to make us look like tyrants. But we're not. And that drives me crazy.

At one point she got very upset and said that I was always angry at her. And I realized that, yeah, my main emotion recently has been anger. She was doing tons of stuff that annoyed the hell out of me and that made me angry.

One example is her attitude towards her mother and me. She often expresses anger at us that we don't have better jobs that pay more. Why did I not work when she was little? Why did we leave New York City? Why don't I work harder and make more money? Why don't I go to the big fancy grocery store across town instead of our local grocery store? Why don't we manage our money better so we can buy more things for her? When I explain that we consciously downsized our careers so we could spend time with our kids, she rolls her eyes.

Where does this come from? We are very antimaterialist. We drive old cars, shop at thrift stores, and have specifically tried to foster in our kids the sense that money and material things aren't the most important things in life. Part of her attitude is probably because starting in sixth grade she's been going to school that, even though it's a public school, has lots of kids who are very affluent, whose parents are very materialistic. But I had hoped we had instilled these values in her that would inoculate her against that kind of materialism. And while I think she understands where we are coming from, these kinds of attacks hurt, mainly I suppose because it seems to show that she might be turning into the kind of materialistic, classist person I really don't like.

She's also got a sense that it's fun to be "provocative." So when we're in a restaurant or other public place she'll loudly start espousing very conservative and offensive political positions in ways that really push our buttons, hoping to get a rise out of us. But for some reason that really bothers me. I know I should just brush it aside, and I do suggest that we switch to another topic of conversation, but she keeps going, and it really makes me mad. Does she really believe this stuff? When she's doing this, I'm not sure. Overall I'm pretty sure that she doesn't, and that she's just "arguing" for argument's sake. But on the other hand, she gets mad that I shop at our local grocery store because it's a "ghetto store"; she refuses to go there, and of course won't even consider applying for a job there. This kind of stuff really makes me despair.

We've also gotten somewhat stricter with her after an incident a few months ago that involved a very large quantity of alcohol. I have to admit I was really surprised, because I thought she had much better judgment and common sense. She claims she learned her lesson, but I felt at the time that we needed to be more vigilant than we had been. And of course, that played into her sense of being a victim and of us being so strict. Over the past couple of weeks I've loosened up, in part because I remembered when I was sixteen, and realized that at that age there's really only so much parents can do. I also do think she learned her lesson about alcohol. And she admits that our concerns about her riding in cars driven by other teens is valid. But I still feel like she needs some guidance, that we can't just let her go off and do anything she wants without any limits at all. She'll have plenty of time to do that after she leaves home . . . Yet she continues to berate us for being the strictest parents in the world, though I know that can't be true, because friends of ours claim that they have been awarded that title by their own kids.

She's also sometimes just plain rude to us, even when we've done something for her, or have gone out of our way to help her out.

Finally, she's very mean to her little brother, making cruel comments, picking arguments with him. That really breaks my heart. And it also means that whenever we are all together, it tends to degenerate into arguing and squabbling between them—because he takes her bait and they end up escalating.

So these are some examples. In general, she often manages to turn situations into something where she's the victim and we are mean/clueless/tyrannical. It really hurts.

But on the other hand, sometimes, she can revert to her wonderful, charming self. Adult friends and relatives who interact with her when we're not around tell us how great she is, how they are so impressed by her. The kids she baby-sits love her. So I know that it's not all bad. But unfortunately, when she's with us, we don't always get to experience the wonderful parts of her personality.

Maybe part of this anger thing is related to my own issues of letting go, of saying goodbye to my little kid, of disappointment that she does things in ways that I don't like. I don't know. Whatever the reason, my emotional responses to her had begun to shrink to the range between annoyed and angry.

So I know that she is at least partly right. I have been reducing everything to anger. I've been becoming a mad dad.

All of these things she's been doing really make me feel hurt, depressed, and disappointed. And I've been expressing those feelings by getting angry. But there's no way I could turn into my dad! I'm a totally different kind of person! When the kids were little I was cuddling and loving and nurturing. Now though, in the face of my daughter's tirades, I find myself unable to deal with this, I don't have the words or emotional tools to talk to her about this. I feel like my mind is going to break or something. It makes me so sad I lay awake at night.

And you know what, this has made me somewhat more understanding of my own dad. If this stuff is getting to me, with all my awareness of gender dynamics and kids issues, I can only imagine what it did to this guy coming out of a totally traditional, rural background, who was raising five kids on a limited income, saw the world in very patriarchal terms, and grew up in a culture that was so different from the one his kids were living in.

As I think about it, I can also see that my daughter might in part be reacting to how I react. As I get angry, she responds in ways that just further anger me. Maybe we've gotten into a cycle of anger.

The good thing is, even if my daughter is really mad at me and in tears, ten minutes later she'll ask me to come in and watch a video with her, or ask me to look over her homework or explain something, or come in to discuss politics. That's really strange to me. When I was mad at my dad, I didn't talk to him for weeks. And sometimes it's hard for me to put aside my anger so quickly. But I'm trying.

So I'm making efforts to understand myself better. I'm exploring the roots of my annoyances and angers. I'm trying to let go of some things that I'd totally internalized in terms of my expectations. I have to figure out where the limits are, which lines are worth drawing. I'm trying to keep a balance between letting her know the things she needs to do for her own good and future, and letting other things slide, realizing they are not so important, that at sixteen plenty of people are out on their own, realizing that she's basically a great kid and will be an incredible woman in a few years.

So I have to chill and zen and conquer my anger so that I don't end up destroying myself. I don't know how successful I'm going to be. But I have to figure all this stuff out not just for my daughter, but also for the sake of my son, who turns thirteen in a few weeks.

Dazed and Confused
Tomas Moniz

I need help. I'm desperate. I'm even turning to them self-help parenting books with names like *You Be the Boss* and *Take Back Control of Your Family* (note picture with white mother and father and grumpy-looking suburban white boy). I'm looking at them and saying, "Yes! Save me." How far we fall—but when you're desperate, anything's game.

But enough with clichés; let's get to the point—as an anarchist antiauthoritarian father trying to bridge that gap between theory and practice, trying to connect my politics to the practice of living my daily life, I've never met this kinda challenge before. And it feels like I am failing. I mean being vegan in New Mexico with my entire Chicano family holding out a plate full of carne asada saying, "You don't eat what?" was easier. Struggling with the practice of nonmonogamy seemed simpler. Struggling to navigate being a teacher within the cold walls of the classroom was a piece of vegan chocolate cake compared to this. My son. Beautiful. On the verge of manhood. So much energy, so much potential.

Stoned. No, not just stoned. Fucking stoned.

Not doing anything: no school work, no responsibilities around the dog, not caring about skating anymore, just worried about acquiring a new white tee, khaki Dickies, clean white Nikes.

But that's not the worst thing.

Lying about it. That was the clincher. I need serious help. He seemed more comfortable making up extravagant explanations for me than talking to me about his choices, his decisions, his willingness to take the consequences if need be. Instead he would tell me things like this: *No, really, I just took this bud from a friend because I didn't want him to smoke because, you know, drugs are bad.*

Followed by his sad little smile.

Help me!

I was talking through this stuff with a good friend of mine and he chided me asking, "Really what do you expect, him to be all, *'Yo, pops, I'm fixing to roll a fat one with me and my boys, you want in?'"* Now sarcasm aside, he had a point. I pride myself on fostering an environment in which my son and my daughters would be active participants in creating their surroundings, and this worked when every option they had was something I was comfortable with for the most part. "You wanna wear a tank top when it's raining, well, try it and see," or, "You wanna not eat when we're having dinner, then don't expect me to do it all again when you're hungry in a couple hours."

But there was no deception, no dishonesty in any of these situations. Until now.

"Hey dad, I need to stop by my girlfriend's house to pick up my math book I left there." I want him to succeed, so I must help him, I feel. However begrudgingly, I get all the other kids in my car, which I need to jumpstart to get going, drive there, wait an excruciating ten minutes, and then have him come in the car followed by an overpowering smell of patchouli hand soap . . . hmmm. A deep breath in and sure enough: weed. I realize that this was all a ploy to get some *grapes,* as the slang goes in Berkeley High. I ask: does he have pot on him?

"No." He looks dumbfounded, like, why on earth would I think such a thing?

I ask him to empty his pockets—out comes some of the nastiest, weak-ass shank I'd ever seen. I almost asked him how much he paid for this because he got robbed. Then I hear his excuse: "I was wrestling with friends in the field, so it must be grass."

Am I that much of a fool I wonder? Is this what I get for doing what I did to my mom? I just want to ridicule him, chide him for thinking me so gullible. You know, parenting by shame. And then it hits me. This is where politics in action collide with theory, this is the battleground where decisions made now can either reflect the parenting most of us are familiar with: parenting based on hypocrisy, blanket authoritarianism, on guilt, or my decisions can reflect . . . and that's where I'm stuck. Reflect what? How else to handle this, other than those rigid patriarchal static options— yelling, screaming, shaming, threatening? Or worse yet, the banal liberal crap that I hear some people (usually nonparents) rattle off about how they'll let them smoke or even smoke with them. So do I let my son smoke pot any ol' time? Do I say, "No, drugs are bad," like the good ol' *South Park* counselor? I know they're not. I don't smoke pot, but I have, and will certainly do it again. Do I say, "You can do it in your room only," and then have to deal with a stoned son at dinnertime? Nothing sounds good, nothing feels right. Where is my little four-year-old who wants pirate parties and the only thing smoking will be the tip of his little pirate pistol?

But we change. Kids grow up. They make their own decisions and must face the consequences of those decisions on their own. I tell him in the car, "I will talk to you about this later tonight when I'm not so upset." In the meantime I remind myself that I don't have all the answers. That this is so much more complex than just him smoking pot or lying or trust. I also remind myself that my responsibility is first and foremost to let him know I love him unconditionally. I don't want my anger or my disappointment to pervade my other interactions with him. After being flat-out lied to like a fool, I still must make him dinner, sit and eat with him and my daughters in a respectful and supportive environment. This sounds obvious or simple, but it is probably the most difficult thing I have to do. To keep these things separate: my anger at one thing and my behavior to him in other areas. To not ridicule him when he comes into the kitchen announcing, "Man, am I hungry," by saying, "Well, that's what you get when you're a fucking pot-head," or something like, "It's called the munchies, stoner."

So what are my responsibilities? Where do they end and his begin? When we do finally talk, I decide first to just ask some questions and then just listen, not blame, guilt, threaten, ignore, dismiss him, his feelings, or his actions. I ask: "Do you like it? How's it make you feel? Do you think it affects you negatively in any way? Do you know what might happen if you get caught with it on BART, in school, buying or selling? Do you want to know my experiences with it?" We talk like this a few times over the next couple of days.

I still don't know what to do and I still feel lost, so I finally try to figure out what I feel I need as a parent, what I feel my responsibilities are, and just what my concerns or fears are. I tell him I don't want him doing it, and I don't think it is helping him succeed in the choices he's made for himself at this point. I tell him of my fear about how this society is ready to pounce on young men, criminalize them and their actions, and that he's already been caught for graffiti and shoplifting (*did pot cause this?* I laugh to myself) and soon he will be out of options. I reiterate that he needs to make his own decisions and he needs to deal with the consequences. I kinda wanna use my line I used when I saw him looking at pornography, "If you old enough to watch it, you old enough to talk about it." Openly and honestly. So I need him to be honest with me, to not deceive me. If I ask him, he should be truthful. Part of the consequences of his actions is owning them, regardless of people's reactions, even his father's. I tell him that being honest doesn't mean he has no privacy. He is his own person and knows what is expected of him. If he can balance doing what he needs to do, with the other choices he wants to make, great. If he can't, then we need to rework our system; we need to question both what I expect and his choices. If we can be honest with each other now, we can learn to understand, support, disagree with each other while still maintaining our autonomy and our connection.

However, none of that will make walking into my son's room with him sitting on the bed stoned out of his mind with Mickey D wrappers about the floor any fucking easier.

A Letter to My Son on His Seventeenth Birthday
Tomas Moniz

Dear Dylan,

It seems so cliché to say that this letter is difficult, but it is; this is the most difficult thing I've ever tried to write partly because I love you so much and am so proud of you and so badly want to show you off to everyone I meet. But unfortunately parenting is a little more complex than loving you fiercely; if that were it, I'd be the best damn dad around.

Soon it will be your birthday. You'll be seventeen. I was thinking of what to get you, trying to stick with something you might want instead of what I wanted to give you; immediately, I knew: the new PlayStation Three with at least five games, two controllers and some exorbitant memory stick; hell, for what that'll cost I might as well get you that car with twenty-two-inch rims you always talking about. And then right as I'm thinking this, I start to get irritated with you. Typical it seems of our interactions lately.

So then I began to fantasize about what I could give you if I had something like an heirloom to pass on to you from father to son as you move from childhood to manhood kinda like that watch in *Pulp Fiction*, the one that he hid up his ass for ten years. But then I remembered I don't wear a watch and neither do you and I don't really have any heirlooms. But there was that story that came with the watch. That's it! Who needs a watch, when you've got a story? Perhaps what I can give you as you prepare to begin your own adult adventure is the story of your birth, remind you where you came from, what life was like back in the day. But don't worry; I'll buy you something as well.

I was three years older than you are now when I found out I was going to be a father. I remember not even really getting what that meant because I had no intention of getting a full-time job or of marrying your mother, though I loved her passionately. I basically had no idea what being a father entailed, what it took, what sacrifices it called for. I was still figuring out how to be myself.

We found out your mom was pregnant in our studio apartment in San Pedro. After your mother peed on it, she couldn't look at the little pregnancy test that I tried to steal because we were so broke but your mom wouldn't let me. She ran from the bathroom and waited on the bed. I lay there with her too for a while until I knew it was time to check. Then, only I went in. There was a moment that I knew she was pregnant and she didn't yet. I sat in that bathroom and time just stopped; the world seemed so detached. I realized my life had changed even though I had just started it. And suddenly there I was on a toilet seat staring at a positive pregnancy test with a woman I just met six months earlier in the next room.

Back then, I was not much different than you are now, loved sports, loved being with friends, loved being young and strong and male, not in any blatantly sexist way but just in that privileged way of believing the world was mine (which of course is rule number one of male privilege, but that knowledge comes later). And then your mother walked in the bathroom with a look of both terror and excitement on her face. Your mom, a young woman I was just getting to know, the person with whom I would become a man, blossoming into my role as partner and as father.

Of course all this would come. But at that moment I was just hella scared. What was I going to tell my mom and my pops? I felt like I was gonna get in trouble.

Initially we talked about abortion, which she didn't want to do. Then we talked about and decided upon adoption. I remember we put those poor prospective adoptive parents through the ringer. We read their profiles, their stories, their attitudes towards open adoption and we chose a couple that we both liked who were young, were smart, and were a lot like me and your mother—only about ten years older and not pregnant. But then they said one thing. One thing: "You don't really want to see him for the first few years, right?"

Your mom and I sat by the pool the next afternoon in her dad's Reseda apartment building, and I remember saying to her. "You know we can just keep the baby. We could do this ourselves." And we did. And we never looked back.

We couldn't because not three weeks later, we were in a room at Santa Barbara hospital, a week after finding a place to live, a day after your mom taught me how to pin on cloth diapers (I had never even seen a cloth diaper before). We were about to have you. We found ourselves walking the halls at two in the morning exhausted, delirious, excited for you to join us.

Your mother got so high on pain killers she kept talking about KitchenAid appliances to describe her pain, and I was so out of it from lack of sleep that I was able to engage her in a dialogue about Cuisinarts and blenders as if it all made perfect sense to me. "I know just what it feels like, honey, to have a toaster-oven-type contraction."

We hehehehe'd and hahahaha'd for a while more and then you joined us (yes, I'm making it a bit simpler than it actually was); with the smell of womb and the musky amniotic fluid flooding the room, I welcomed you into the world crying harder than I have ever cried in my life.

Three days later, I drove to the store for lunch and stopped just as I pulled out of our driveway. What had I become, what was my life going to become, and who was that person back there, waiting for me, needing me? I decided there in the road that I was now a father; not any father, your father.

After that, I took you everywhere. No errand was too stressful, no place too child-unfriendly. I was coming, I was a father and you were the best damn kid a man like me could ever have. You were (and still are) precocious, funny, crazy, full of life. You were always at my side. I remember changing your diaper on my feminist studies teacher's desk, laying in the sand with you waiting for your mother to come home from school, or putting you in a pot with various vegetables sticking out and me, your mom, and a good friend staring at you like dinner. We sent that picture as our Christmas card to relatives. My mom was not pleased.

Writing this I realize how much of my early twenties were dedicated to you, and seeing you now seventeen, taller than me, so busy with life, feeling like the world is yours, I am not sure how to both hold on and celebrate your eminent departure.

And then I found this.

The other day I was cleaning out my office at school and something was tucked up in this drawer. I pulled it out. It was a gift from you when you were in the fourth grade. It was a memento you gave me to remember you by. You made it one day when I brought you to work. You'd sit beside me. You loved the stapler. You stapled page after page, using staples like glue. Anyways, you stapled your school picture to what I halfheartedly said was my favorite Pokemon character after you pestered me to choose one of your like three thousand cards you had collected. Your staples held, for there it was, still together: your smiling face and Lickitung. It must be eight years ago you did that.

And so this letter is my memento to you; it might not mean much now (did I just tuck your gift away minutes after you gave it to me?) but one day, one far away day, you will look at this and smile and remember what it was like being my son and perhaps you'll pick up the phone and call your old man.

Dylan, here is my small gift to you.

Love, your father

Section Four

POLITICS OF PARENTING: GENDER, RACE, ALLIES, VISIONS

A Kid-Friendly Wild Rumpus
Tomas Moniz

I was twenty and about to be a father. He had just turned twenty-one and was on his way to Redwood Summer, a call for people to come participate in direct action to save the redwoods and old growth forests of Northern California. We ran into each other at the local hardware store. It was May 1990. We had been friends during the school year in Santa Barbara, studying together, attending environmental meetings on campus, talking politics—and like many college students, becoming more radical. We had fantasized in hushed tones during class breaks what it would be like to join hundreds of others attempting to make a change. But as the spring quarter came to a close, we saw less of each other. He was planning on participating in Redwood Summer; I was planning on preparing our small home for our first child.

So there we were standing in a hardware store aisle; it had been a couple weeks since we last talked. He was holding a backpack full of stuff for a road trip. I was holding a bag of supplies to baby-proof the electrical sockets in my house. He was picking things in preparation to camp out for weeks. I was going to pick up a few more shifts at the used bookstore that I worked for to help with the bills over the summer.

I remember the look on his face when he asked for the last time, "Can't you just leave the baby with your lady for awhile; they'll both be here when you get back, but, right now, the earth needs you—right now, not when your child's eighteen or nineteen."

Now despite all the ways that this statement is fucked up, it's painful for me to admit that it almost worked. I saw Redwood Summer as my big chance, my opportunity to do something more. I feared that the pending birth of my son would be an impediment to my abilities to participate in creating social change. Up north in the trees: that's where the action was, not singing lullabies and changing diapers.

And so I squirmed and gave some lame excuse about how I would love to go but that my lady won't let me. Pathetic to blame family, to see it as a burden. But I did.

Now as much as I hold myself responsible for those former attitudes, and I do, I believe there is a larger issue also at fault. As a burgeoning radical, I was surrounded by a mythology of revolution that celebrated only one way to be a revolutionary; and, believe me, there were no newborn infants involved.

So at the time, I felt cheated at having to miss this event because of my other responsibilities; I mean all my radical role models seemed to have chosen otherwise. Cuban revolutionary Che Guevara (and who didn't love Che at twenty?) left his kids behind and wrote oft-quoted, eloquent letters home. Ulrike Meinhof, who haunted my dreams as one of the few revolutionaries who had kids and chose to commit herself anyways, had to send her children into hiding and then sever connections with them entirely. My Chicano icons, Joaquin Murrieta or Gregorio Cortez, didn't saddle up with their two-year-olds. In the *corridos* about them, there were only guns, whiskey, and getaways.

None of the stories my friend and I shared about radical politics included parents or children or grandparents or safe spaces.

So my friend left for the redwoods, and I remained.

I went on to evolve my notions of fatherhood with the help of my partner and through reading and studying and working to create a small community of like-minded parents. But during those first few years, I secretly dreamed of the chance to once again be "able" to participate like a "true" revolutionary. The mythology of the revolutionary created a chasm between what I was "doing" and what was "important." Someday, I consoled myself, I could return to the fray, just as soon as I got the kids to bed.

So I longed for the road to the next demonstration even as I worked to create a childcare cooperative in my neighborhood. I imagined campfires in the forests of Northern California while I changed diapers on my feminist studies teacher's desk. I dreamed of delivering fiery orations as I read *Where the Wild Things Are* over and over to my son, both of us yelling, "Let the wild rumpus begin!" However, it finally dawned on me: why the hell couldn't there be a kid-friendly wild rumpus?

And, yes, I know there were parents who have been able to participate in various forms of resistance throughout history (a testament, I'd bet, to the people who surrounded them). I have even had powerful support from my family to dedicate time, energy, and finances to various projects. So it can be done. But it shouldn't be so daunting, so isolating. I sometimes dream about what might have happened had my friend encouraged me to come with my lady and my baby. Perhaps I still would not have gone. Or perhaps I would have. Perhaps someone else like me would have. Perhaps a bunch of us would have. If the entire event was kid-friendly, family-friendly, with various actions and spaces, some of which, of course, could be more "direct" than others. But the possibilities, the potential, seem unlimited.

Many people have embraced the mythology of revolutionaries and activists who left their families behind, so total was their commitment. But how about a new mythology, one that celebrates revolutionaries who refuse to leave anyone behind and refuse to remain silent? If I have learned anything, I have learned this: whatever we are involved in, it should take into account the ability for multigenerational participation. That's sustainability, that's revolutionary, that's the prefigurative politics I want to commit myself to.

My son is now nineteen; I am at peace and, in fact, grateful for the choices I have made. Looking back over the time that has elapsed, I have no regrets. I often wonder what my friend is doing. I want to ask him how that summer turned out. What was climbing those tall trees like? What craziness happened around the campfires? Did he fall in love with a little earth mama like we joked about? I'd also like to thank him: He was one of many people who have inspired and revolutionized me.

In fact, when I think about being a radical parent, I remember fondly all the strange, amazing people that I've met in this loose-knit diverse thing we call a radical community: the ones who organize anarchist conferences with childcare and parenting panels, the mamas and papas writing zines and the allies who buy them, the infoshop volunteers who do it year after year, the anarchist parenting listservs with their thoughtful reflections on how to parent in radical ways, the wandering crusties I encounter as I travel, sometimes alone, sometimes with my children, the artists who plan midnight mystery murder bike rides, and the strangers in distant cities who welcome me into their homes.

Because whether I'm home or on the road, whether I'm with my children or not, I am always a parent as well as a radical, and I will not be silent about demanding we consider ways to include everyone. And when I'm old, I want to embellish stories of my swarthy figure, similar to the Chicano banditos of old, only instead of the reins of a horse I am cupping the palm of my child.

And maybe a bottle of tequila.

Five Questions for Profeminist Fathers
Jeremy Adam Smith

*I*n 2008, *Australian feminist blogger Blue Milk posted "10 questions on feminist motherhood," which inspired me to adapt her questions for fathers on my blog* Daddy Dialectic. *Here are five of my answers.*

1. What has surprised you most about fatherhood?

In college, I was active with many feminist and profeminist organizations. After college, I was in a stable, monogamous relationship and in my work with various progressive nonprofits, I usually had solid, respectful relationships with female coworkers. I watched guy coworkers get into trouble for sexist remarks or actions (inadvertent and otherwise), but that never happened to me and my policy was to duck and cover if it turned into a major issue.

Every once in a while, a female coworker would even go out of her way to tell me how refreshingly nonsexist I was—"When Jeremy talks to me, he never looks at my breasts," said one person, whose breasts I did, in fact, secretly glance at once or twice. These pats on the head were always reassuring and contributed to a decade-long mood of complacency about gender issues.

Then I became a dad. And I was shocked by the degree to which my now-habitual commitment to feminist values was put to the test. In fact, habits went out the window; everything took conscious effort, as if I'd had an intellectual and emotional stroke and needed to learn how to walk and talk all over again.

Most shocking of all, I think the power in our relationship started to inexorably tilt in my direction, as perhaps it always did, as we became parents. Even when I took time off of paid work to serve as my son's primary caregiver, the tilt continued. It didn't seem, and still doesn't seem, to matter what I want or decide—I just keep growing more powerful in the relationship.

What do I mean by power? In this context, we might say it's the ability to do and say what we want and need to do or say. From this perspective, we've both lost power: Parenthood constrains our choices in countless ways, which I don't think I need to explain to other parents.

But there is no question, absolutely none, that my wife has lost more power than I have. This won't surprise moms who are reading this, but it certainly surprised me.

The biggest reason for this, I would say, is that I have simply not been as absorbed by the physical and emotional demands of caregiving, even when I was primary caregiver; and at this writing, I am the one who is making most of the money and feels most driven to advance in my so-called career.

Mind you, I have been *vastly* more involved with care than many other fathers and I have explicitly designed my work situation to be flexible. And yet it is still the case—this is the important thing, the most important thing that needs to be said—that parenthood has diminished my wife's power. Or, to put it a different way, constrained her ability to make choices.

2. How have your profeminist values changed over time? What is the impact of fatherhood on your profeminism?

Think about the implications: If a guy like me—who has every good intention and a history of profeminist activism, and who even served a stint as a stay-at-home dad—is failing at the task for forging an egalitarian family, then what does that tell us about the prospects of wider social change?

Some people reading this probably think they have this one all figured out. They'll say I was naïve for ever even imagining that equality in one family was possible—what we need, they'll argue, is nothing less than the overthrow of white-supremacist capitalist patriarchy. Only after the revolution can our piddling interpersonal relationships be lastingly altered.

Before becoming a father, I was one of those people.

And so I never thought utopia in one family was possible; I was really just trying to muddle through, as I still am. Here's the thing: Most of the people I'm talking about aren't parents—and the ones who are, are not what I would call dedicated parents. In fact, too often left-wing activists and leaders neglect their family responsibilities, especially the guys.

Am I judging them? Sure, a bit—the fathers, anyway—but mainly as a warning to myself and others. They're workaholics in the service of social change, as I once was, and I suspect that they will regret the things they missed just as much as their corporate counterparts.

As a result, the problems parents face are all very abstract to them. They don't see, they can't, how vital and immediate it is for heterosexual couples to establishing a domestic division of labor that makes both parties happy. They have no idea—I had no idea, before becoming a parent—how difficult and urgent it is for fathers and mothers to figure this one out.

It's all very well to talk about universal health care and parental leave and so on—but who will take the baby to the doctor? What do you say when a breastfeeding mother just wants to stay home and take care of her baby? Do you condemn her, as some have done, for being insufficiently feminist? Or do you say society and the economy made her do it, thereby denying the importance of her perception of what she needs and what the baby needs?

And what about the fathers? Are their feelings and needs irrelevant? What happens when a father yearns to stay home with his child, but can't, because his wife wants to be the one to do that and he has to earn the money? Or what if he does stay home, and spends his days feeling like a fish out of water? No social movement can help him; feminism can tell him that he's doing the right thing—God knows, nothing else in our culture will—but that won't matter much to the average stay-at-home dad. He mainly needs a supportive community as well as role models.

Here's something I think progressive feminist folks need to understand in a deep way: Parents aren't soldiers. We don't take marching orders. And none of us is a general. You can't tell your partner what she should want out of life, even, perhaps especially, when her decisions make you more powerful in the relationship. You can't control the way the world thinks of you, and you don't get to say what social and economic conditions you'll face as a parent. This breeds feelings of helplessness, powerlessness, anger.

At the end of the day, your main task is to survive and support your family and raise happy children; how you respond to the things you can't control reveals a great deal about your character, some of it good and some of it bad. You might discover (have you noticed my retreat to the safety of the second person?) a capacity for sacrifice and care that you never knew was there.

On the flip side, the dark one, you might also find yourself erupting with petty rage and misdirected resentment, eruptions that frighten you, your child, and your partner. In those scary moments, when our worst emotions take over and drive our ideals and aspirations over a cliff, it is easiest of all for both fathers and mothers to fall back on traditional patterns of dominance and submission.

What does that have to do with feminism? Everything, and nothing.

Pledging allegiance to feminist ideals doesn't make you a good person or a good parent or a good partner, but it might remind you of the power you have—we always have power, if only over ourselves—and the need to restrain that power or share it with other people. It can also remind fathers of something that I think is crucial: There are alternatives; you do have choices, and your choices matter. You don't have to be the man your father was; you don't have to be the idiots we see on TV; you can be a new kind of man, and you can help your sons become that kind of man.

3. What makes your fathering profeminist? How does your approach differ from an antifeminist father's?

At the start, I saw participating in infant care as being the most important thing I could do to make my fathering profeminist, and maybe that was correct—it had the merit of being a pretty straightforward mission. I did my best.

And that's a fundamentally different framework than the one an antifeminist or nonfeminist father brings to fatherhood—for the best of them, fatherhood involves an uncomplicated commitment to breadwinning above all else, which, whatever its shortcomings, is definitely an important role to fulfill; for the worst of them, fatherhood becomes another opportunity to dominate women and expand their egos. On this front, I don't sell myself or profeminist fathers short: A commitment to care is crucial, and makes a real difference for mothers and children.

I also think a commitment to profeminist fathering leads in a very direct way to supporting profeminist public policies:

antidiscrimination policies, subsidized daycare and preschool, universal health care, paid parental leave, and so on. Enacting these policies will provide a nurturing context for our personal decisions and make profeminist fathering more likely to flourish. That's another difference between a consciously profeminist and a nonfeminist father: There's a political dimension to your fathering that, I think, must be expressed through voting, activism, writing, and, ultimately, public policy.

4. When have you felt compromised as a profeminist father? Do you ever feel you've failed as a profeminist father?

At this point, I'm compromised *every freaking day*; I fail *every single day*. This is not false modesty. The commitment to infant care was straightforward, though in retrospect I see those halcyon days as a simpler time. As the years have gone by, I've fallen further and further short of my ideals, and profeminist fathering has started to look increasingly complicated to me.

I confess that I feel really quite lost when it comes to applying profeminist values to my relationships with my wife and my son as they are right now. From that perspective, this is an awkward time for me to tackle these questions—I'm struggling toward the answers but don't yet have good ones, and it's possible that I never will.

5. Do you feel feminism has failed fathers and, if so, how? Personally, what do you think feminism has given fathers?

"Feminism" is, of course, not monolithic.

I would say that individual feminist thinkers and leaders have certainly failed fathers, in the sense that they have behaved as though fathers don't matter or don't exist or can only serve a purely oppressive role within the family. Another group of feminists has actually attacked the emergence of caregiving dads—I submit the philosopher Linda Hirshman as an example.

But I would describe those two groups as a minority; I think a majority of feminists can foresee a positive role for fathers and, indeed, desperately want to see fatherhood redefined in a positive and progressive way. I don't think feminism has offered a well-articulated vision of fatherhood, but that's OK: It really falls to fathers to redefine fatherhood.

This is the great thing that feminism has given fathers: Its success has triggered culture-wide dialogues among men about what a good father should be and do. Feminists themselves are not always comfortable with these arguments, and certainly there has been much to criticize.

But, as an old New Leftist once said, revolutions don't happen in velvet boxes. They're messy, contradictory, sometimes downright revolting—but usually also thrilling and necessary. Women have been rising for over a century, and only recently have men started to really change in response. From that perspective, it's an exciting time.

This leads me to another thing that has surprised me about fatherhood and feminism: In a perverse way, fatherhood has strengthened my commitment to feminism. By revealing the limits of my good intentions and scope of action, fatherhood has pushed me to seek new answers to feminist questions I thought I had answered in my early twenties, on both personal and political levels.

Fatherhood has also reminded me, in a visceral way, of the inequalities that persist between men and women, and, in particular, the burdens carried by mothers. Those burdens and inequalities shape and poison our most intimate relationships whether we want them to or not.

Here again, feminism is useful for fathers and mothers: It gives us perspective, or it should.

It's easy to be overcome by day-to-day difficulties and despair of the possibility of changing the balance of power between men and women. But if we lift our eyes and look at the sweep of the past through feminism's eyes, we can see that the balance of power *has* changed, on this and many other fronts. History doesn't stop just because we personally feel stuck. If we look at the lives of the people who came before us, we see that our actions in the present do matter, both our individual choices and the act of speaking out in public.

Finally, returning to question two, fatherhood has changed my relationship with feminism in one other way: If I speak out now, it is with a lot more sadness and less righteousness than I did when I was a college student. At this point, I've failed so many times that I can hardly denounce others for their imperfections.

But I still feel like we as fathers need to speak out, even if it's just to friends or through blogs or zines with a few hundred readers. The alternative is silence—but worse than that, meaninglessness. If I'm going to fail, the failure has to mean something. It has to be recorded (if only for myself), examined, put to use, leveraged, transmuted. Feminism gives us a way to do that, to transform our private pains into social change.

Losing the Battle, Winning the War
Tomas Moniz

I've come to believe that parenting is a losing battle.

We have weapons, secret and dirty, imperfect and volatile. These weapons are, of course, ourselves, and our faith, and our hope, and our trust, in each other and our children.

I ran into a friend on the street, someone who loves and vouches for my son even when, at times, I don't. We chitchatted for a minute, discussed the fact that my son did graduate high school regardless of his 1.3 GPA, and then we started talking about the fact that he had been in a couple of fights recently. That's when she jokingly asked a question, a seemingly innocent one, not meant to be malicious in any way, but a question that sat with me for a while, that bothered me: *How did such a feminist father raise such a typical boy?* This of course alluded to a ton of other questions and assumptions: that we can control our children's actions, or worse, that their actions are somehow a direct reflection of ourselves. Or that there is a typical "boyness" which is at odds with typical "feminism." Or that perhaps I wasn't even a feminist in the first place. Basically, the question assumes that I had failed. Needless to say I responded with some typically articulate response like: *Yeah, I know, huh. Go figure*. But really, how could I answer this?

Can you be a feminist father when your son gets into fights resulting in an inch-and-a-half wound on his forehead the day of his prom or when he uses homophobic language to explain why he doesn't like something? What's it say about your parenting when, despite your best intentions at surrounding your youngest aspiring-singer-of-a-daughter with kick-ass female musical role models, she openly dotes on various prefabricated teen pop star variations? Have you lost your radical credentials when your other daughter who seems destined for athletic and/or artistic glory, puts that talent to use creating outfits from H&M and designing her own personal makeup chamber/beauty parlor in her mother's extra bathroom. The horror, the horror . . .

I read someplace that the amount of time our kids spend under our influence is a fraction of the time our kids will spend under the influence of the media and society. They might spend more time with YouTube than you; in their busy lives running from school, to friends, to practices, to entertainment, where do you fit in? And most likely, you are doing just as much if not more running around. Talk about being outnumbered and outgunned. Sometimes I wish I could just make the world stop! Thinking about this makes me terrified, mortified, desperate to do something: lose the TV, homeschool, read and listen to everything first before their little susceptible minds got a hold of something.

But that is parenting based on fear, on a lack of trust, on misguided notions of perfection. I am not perfect. I'm flawed and my parenting is too, but in our hubris is our redemption. We can make amends in the processing of those contact zones at which my values come in to conflict with other values, and then those conflicts are made gloriously or painfully visible to my children.

In his book *White Like Me*, Tim Wise succinctly stated the situation: "The power of resistance is to set the example: not necessarily to change the person with whom you disagree, but to empower the one who is watching and whose growth is not yet complete, whose path is not at all clear, whose direction is still very much up in the proverbial air." Our children are our witnesses, and we must remind ourselves of that. Remember that it is they who will testify about us in the future. So yeah, my kids see all these messages out in the world, out on my block, and shit, sometimes in my own damn house (why do I keep playing the latest Lady Gaga song over and over in front of my kids?!) but they see our resistance as well, the moments we challenge others and ourselves, our celebrations honoring the diverse and multifaceted beauty of the world, how we hold and love each other despite our anger, how we support and nurture those in our lives and in our communities.

When we censor, it actually takes away the opportunities for dialogue, for growth, for learning.

But yes—letting go like that makes parenting feel like a lost cause. There is nothing wrong with recognizing that feeling. For me, the acknowledgement of the seemingly insurmountable odds ironically inspires me or allows me to lighten up. I realize that all I can do is be the example of leading a life the way I think I should: critical yet communal, driven to be an active member, to be the change I want to see in the world. Man, I hate it when I'm a cliché.

Now all this doesn't mean we don't actively and directly fight to protect our kids but it does mean we have to let them go even while they're young trusting we've given them the skills, the tools, yes, even the weapons effective enough for them to fight on after we've lost the battle. Fight on for themselves.

Trust in them is perhaps the most important weapon.

So if I could answer my friend's question now I'd say: *Yes, I am a feminist father, a rad dad, a militant antiracist. But that's me. My kids will choose their own paths and I have to trust them to do so. On their own time. In their own way.*

But of course that doesn't mean that while they're with me, they don't wake up to a little Nina Simone or Le Tigre, be quasi-forced to attend anarchist book fairs, shop at thrift stores. They fight sometimes; they resist, as they should. But then I hear one singing the chorus from "Rebel Girl," see one drawing designs and cutting clothes she bought at Goodwill to make her own fashion, even hear my son explain to his friend without a moment of hesitation who the EZLN are and what they believe: *They believe,* he says, *another way is possible. They believe the battle might be lost at times, but the war for our hearts will be won together.*

I believe the same thing.

Doing the Wrong Thing
Is Better than Doing Nothing
Tomas Moniz

Parenting has taught me a lot about dealing with things I'd rather not deal with. I've been forced to breathe deeply and make the call to the doctor at three in the morning: *Um, my daughter won't stop crying*, and when the doctor asks why she's crying, I've had to confess, *Well, I kinda dropped her on her head today.*

That never feels good to admit to.

Or I've had to clench my mouth shut tightly and just let my daughter have her feelings, be disappointed, resist the urge to placate her, to try to "make" her feel better by saying something inane like, *Well your little ten-year-old friend who won't share with you is a jerk.*

Definitely, not good parental role modeling.

I've also learned to deal with larger, seemingly inhuman bureaucratic systems such as institutionalized schooling with all its rules and policies that seem to believe learning only takes place in a classroom. No, I don't think it's fair that my seventh-grader gets an F in classes because I took her on a trip to see a sick relative. I've learned to face a police and justice system that views children and particularly teenaged men as criminals first and foremost.

Parenting, however, has also demonstrated that there are the choices we need to make between letting some things slide while focusing on others.

My daughter, arriving home ten minutes later than she said she would, might be OK now and then. I can raise an eyebrow and shrug off her *What, the bus was late* exasperated remark when I ask why she's not on time. Because when she's out at night and forgets to call when I explicitly explained that I expected her to, that ain't something you can let slide. It's something you have to address, and it's difficult to hold her to the agreed upon consequences. It's painful to hear her anger, her frustration, to be the target of her unmitigated teenage rage. And that shit's scary.

However, this is not an essay about my children.

Let me stop stalling.

A friend of mine was arrested for domestic violence. There's a story there. There are reasons for his anger and even empathy around the whole situation: towards him, towards his partner. The whole affair is sad. In the end, perhaps it will all be for the best for both of them and their kids.

But there is no excuse for violence in a relationship.

None.

Ever.

The crisis is over. She's moved out of their home. They have a routine set up. Things are almost back to normal. People in my circle of friends are even joking about it.

And that is what bothers me, what makes me uncomfortable.

I started to ask around: what is my role in all this now? How do I address this with my daughters and son? How to be a true friend?

I don't want to be the one to constantly bring it up every time I see him, but I also don't want a "business as usual"–type friendship, a "don't ask, don't tell" relationship because that is so much easier: pretend it never happened.

I remember when the Chris Brown and Rihanna incident occurred. I immediately talked to my kids about it, especially my youngest daughter who was very into both of them. I asked how they felt about hearing the news. I didn't want to let this opportunity slip: a chance to address the unacceptability of domestic violence, to establish a clear "zero-tolerance" policy.

Some things can slide; physical and emotional abuse can't.

But what to do with my friend? Why did this feel so much more difficult?

Soon after all this happened, I spoke with another friend of mine, a woman, a person who had been in an abusive relationship in the past, and she gave me some advice I hold dearly now. She said when she was going through it, that she wished people would have done something, anything. She looked at me and stated: *Sometimes doing the wrong thing is better than doing nothing.*

I understood immediately that that was why I was so uncomfortable. I could see how easy doing nothing could have been.

Denial is powerful. But as parenting has taught me: some things can slide but sometimes you have to face it.

I knew I needed to talk to him before he moved off the block, so one night when he came over to borrow something, I did.

We stood out on my stoop, and I expressed my anger and disappointment. I told him I knew it would be work, but that I wanted to be the kind of friend who is willing to both stand up for someone and to hold them accountable. I expressed my concerns about how he was taking responsibility for his actions.

I did, however, acknowledge that I had no answers, only questions. But I told him I'm willing to struggle to find those answers with him, together.

We hugged, and he left.

A few days later, I raised the subject again with my daughters and my twenty-year-old son who was visiting. He heard all about it from his mom and his sisters. Everyone was arguing over it. Gossiping about it. In fact, my youngest daughter and I saw the cop cars in front of their house when it happened and I said to her almost in jest, *I hope that's not what I think it is.* I cringe thinking about how uncritical a statement that is in regards to domestic abuse.

So we were all sitting around the table, my two daughters and my son eating dinner. I confessed, *I am angry that I don't know what to do or say. I feel like a hypocrite ridiculing Chris Brown, and yet when it happens on my street I'm at a loss as to what I should do. Just because I'm a friend with someone doesn't mean they're not accountable, you know.*

My youngest daughter shook her head and said finally, *You know it's not your fault, Dad,* as if I was acting foolish.

Getting chastised by your kids is another thing you learn how to deal with from parenting.

However, it was then that I realized I was looking at my son sitting across from me. He was looking at me.

It dawned on me that I haven't had a conversation like this with him in a long time. As a man. As a person who might disagree with me, who might not see it the way I do. I was terrified.

My son remained silent for a moment, looked at his sisters and then back at me, and finally said, *I know, Dad, I know,* and he looked me in the eye, *that shit is totally fucked up.*

Not the most eloquent response, but it was clear that he meant it.

It was one of the most reassuring moments in my life. It's strange to love this young person so much, and for years feeling like I could control or at least strongly influence his actions. Now he stands taller than me, muscular, lean, a man, and I have no control over anything anymore in his life (well, except for kicking in money for his rent), and yet I still have such expectations of him. And I know he will let me down in the future, will make mistakes in relationships and in life, but hearing him say that with such conviction, without equivocation, in front of his sisters was a profound moment for me.

As the weeks pass, I still bring it up with my daughters now and then. In fact, now, my middle child has a boyfriend. I see how quickly I will have little control in her life as well. It's hard to let go. But I'm gonna do it. With love and with encouragement and with trust.

They taught me that.

I will not let things slide anymore and this is a lesson I dedicate to all those who are victims of violence: from the batons or gun barrels of the police, because of the words and intimidation of bullies, or even at the hands of their own family.

I promise you I will never look the other way.

I promise you I will do something whether it's the right thing or not at the time.

I promise. I will.

Straight on Castro
Jeremy Adam Smith

I was never a great friend of marriage. When I was growing up in a series of east coast and Midwestern suburbs in the 1970s and '80s, the institution of marriage seemed more like a gory roadside smash-up than the loving union of one man and one woman. And as I spent junior high school witnessing the disintegration of my family and of many of the families around me, I was also discovering that boys were boys and girls were girls, and boys who acted like girls were faggots.

You see, when I was a kid in Saginaw, Michigan, I made a horrible mistake: I chose to play the flute in my school band. I was the only boy to do so. And at first, I was just awful. There were twelve chairs, and for the first half of the first year, I was dead last. The girl flutists ignored me. The all-male drum section made it their habit to inflict on me the full range of junior-high-school torments, from tripping me up in gym class to writing "faggot" on my locker in magic marker to straight-up beat-downs. But I persisted in blowing the flute, that silvery phallus.

Do I sound like a rebel? A gender nonconformist? Don't be too impressed. I just never got the memo. Eric Roeder would call my friend Jim Petee a "fag" and Jim would say, "I'm not a fag! You're a fag!" Then Eric would give Jim a push into the locker, and that would be that. But when Eric Roeder called me a fag, I would just shrug. What's a fag? I wondered. I had no idea. I was just a kid, and so was Eric Roeder; I don't think he really knew what a fag was either. I still got pushed into the locker, but, unlike Jim, I just didn't see the problem with the whole "fag" thing.

And yet an undeniable menace lurked inside the word. Being called a "fag" meant that you were weak, an easy target . . . in short, a girl. But the word's true menace, I now realize, arose from its inchoate intimation of sex. Real sex. Fucking. It was more than an insult. "Jerk" was an insult. "Fag" was a cage that boys built around other boys, one that was intended to stand between the alleged fag and true manhood. A boy in the cage would never be permitted to experience the glories of fucking. Instead, he would be fucked. Like a girl. My mistake, my fatal blind spot, was that I didn't see the cage being built. I just wanted to play the flute; I liked the way it sounded and looked. In my sixth-grade naïveté, I didn't realize that it was a girl's instrument and that boys of my age should not play with girly things.

When I finally started to see the bars that divided me from everyone else, I fought back in two ways. First, I started to furiously practice the flute, two to three hours a day. And so one fateful Monday I zoomed past all the girls from last chair to first, and I held that first chair for the rest of my time in the band.

At roughly the same time, I challenged one of the asshole drummers to a fight. I went down in a hail of fists, of course. The next time someone called me a faggot, I threw myself into him as well, arms flailing. I lost that fight, too. In fact, I lost every single battle I was in that year—perhaps twelve in all. Of course I lost: I was a skinny kid who weighed in at a lower class than my opponents.

But ultimately, I won the war. Eric Roeder called me over to his kettledrum one day, like Fonzie calling Potsie and Richie into the bathroom that served as his "office."

"Jeremy," he said. "Why are you always trying to fight me?"

"Because you hassle me all the time," I said, perhaps a bit sullenly.

"So you're just trying to stand up for yourself?" he said, surprised, as though the idea had just come to him that I might try to do this.

"Yeah," I said, dumbfounded. "Of course."

"OK," he said. "Let's not fight." There was no handshake and we certainly never became friends; this is not an after-school special. But after that terse little interaction, the bullying evaporated.

It wasn't just the boys who seemed to gain new respect for me; my fellow flutists finally noticed me, and started talking to me. Michelle Gase, on whom I had a huge crush, even invited me over to her house. I didn't know what to do once I got there, but the journey of one thousand miles begins, my friends, with a single step.

Perhaps it goes without saying that I didn't stop being a geek: the following year, when my friend Colleen communicated my romantic interest directly to Michelle, Michelle reportedly laughed out loud, an event from which I am still recovering. But I had found a comfortable niche in the junior-high-school (and later high-school) social ecology, and it was a niche in which I could thrive on my own terms.

Do you see the lesson I learned, the one that every American boy must learn? The formula is simple: a) dominate the girls and b) fight other boys. It's never good for a boy to do a girly thing, but, if you must, you had better be better at it than any girl, and you had better be willing to punch any boy in the face who says that doing it makes you a girl. This formula worked for me, I am sorry to report. It's worked for millions of American men of my generation. And even as we're were being trained to fear the queer, we were at the same time watching heterosexuality, in the form of our parents' marriages, disintegrate before our very eyes.

My own parents are now divorced, of course, as are virtually all the parents I knew growing up, as are the parents of the mother of my child. Thus it should not surprise anyone that marriage did not seem very desirable to us. Olli and I got together in 1994, lived and traveled together for years, moved to the Mission in San Francisco together in 2000. But in all those years, we never married. We didn't consciously reject marriage, mind you. It just didn't mean very much to us.

When Mayor Gavin Newsom—for whom I did not vote— legalized same-sex marriage in San Francisco in February 2004, I was entirely a bystander. Yet I was still moved by the spectacle of beaming gay and lesbian couples lining up in front of the San Francisco City Hall, sometimes hemmed in on all sides by unpleasant people with ugly signs. Walking by City Hall one afternoon on my way to the library, I saw two slim women dressed in white, sitting on the grass, their hands folded on each other's laps, their foreheads touching. I assumed that they had just been married. For the rest of the day I felt strangely peaceful, perhaps even slightly stoned.

My son was born—after a sixty-minute labor!—in July 2004. And in the months that followed, my resistance to marriage started to melt away. Yes, both Olli and I thought marriage would be convenient, now that we were parents. But in my eyes at least, it was also true that San Francisco's season of same-sex weddings had raised the value of marriage. I remembered that couple in white, sitting in the grass; perhaps I hoped marriage would give me the peace it seemed to give them.

Of course, not everything changed; we still stubbornly rejected the trappings of a traditional wedding. We slunk off to City Hall, our baby son in arms, and "eloped," to use a quaint old word. The judge was a trim, diminutive, mannish woman of late-middle years, and her eyes held a reassuring twinkle that said to me, *Hey, I'm not taking this too seriously either*. I didn't tell my parents; we hardly told anyone. A year later my mother visited and accidentally saw our marriage certificate hanging in the back of my closet. "What?!" she cried. "You got married and didn't tell me?"

She was furious. I just shrugged. It was as though I was thirteen and she had discovered a *Playboy* magazine hidden in my closet.

Marriage didn't much change anything in my life or the way I felt about myself and the world, but parenthood certainly had. By the fall of 2005, our old life had been wrapped up in a dirty diaper and tossed in the trash. There were no more evenings in the Make-Out Room shooting pool and drinking margaritas and dancing and then crawling over to the Latin American for shots and then perhaps to the Elbo Room to see bands with names like Double-Jointed Donkey Dick or Death Valley High.

Instead, I worked part-time and took care of my infant son Liko for most of the day while Olli was at her job. In sunny, desperate playgrounds I taught Liko to walk, his little fists clenched around my aching forefingers. Pushing a swing, I'd eye the mothers and they eyed me, or so I imagined. I was typically the only father. The moms seldom spoke to me and I was frankly afraid of them. I feared—it sounds ridiculous to admit—that if I initiated a real conversation, they'd think I was hitting on them. Deep in my bones, I felt that I didn't belong on weekday playgrounds. Not just because I was a dad; I didn't even feel like a parent, not then. I felt like a spy, an interloper, an anthropologist studying a lost tribe of stroller-pushing urban nomads.

By this time we lived on the border between Noe Valley and the Castro, a mad scientist's laboratory of new family forms, whose representative on the city's Board of Supervisors is a gay man who coparents a biological child with his lesbian best friend. But at first

I didn't realize how many of the other parents on the playground were gay and lesbian; despite the fact I had had many queer friends, at this time I still assumed breeding was what straight people did. And I remember the first time I met Jackie and her smiley toddler Ezra; beckoned by her friendly smile, she was one of the first stay-at-home moms I decided to talk to. Later I saw Ezra with a woman named Jessica, and I thought she was his babysitter.

Wrong. Jessica was one mommy and Jackie was the other. Fortunately, I figured this out before my new friends discovered my ignorance. In time, I met many other families, both gay and straight, and we formed a new kind of child-centered community, one I never expected to have. After we became close, Jessica (the nonbiological mother) told me that it drove her crazy when people assumed she was the nanny, which put her constantly in the position of having to explain her relationship to her own family. Embarrassed, I didn't tell her about my early assumption, and I still haven't told her.

When the California Supreme Court approved same-sex marriage on May 15, 2008, Jackie and Jessica just knew, as soon as they heard, that they would marry. At the wedding, Jackie wore black and she smiled in a way that seemed simultaneously bright and distant; Jessica, who had been stressed for weeks about the wedding, held her face very still, as if afraid that the wrong emotion would slip out. The ceremony was conducted by their close friends Laura and Peter, who is Ezra's biological father and someone Jackie and Jessica consider to be a member of the family.

"I now pronounce you happily married," said Peter, and the two women kissed.

For Jessica's parents, their daughter's marriage was an intensely meaningful event. "It was wonderful to see Jessica so dressed up and looking so beautiful," said Jessica's mother Elizabeth. "I was just so happy for them." Every member of Jackie and Jessica's circle of friends and family that I interviewed felt the same way: It made us happy to see our friends marry. That's a commonplace feeling at weddings, but, of course, not everyone in America has the right to a legal marriage. Their wedding was extraordinary because it came to us all as a gift we never expected.

Not everyone accepted the gift. I know of several same-sex weddings depopulated by the neutron bomb of homophobia.

When Angela and Mary (not their real names) wed, Angela's mother Shirley refused to attend on vaguely religious grounds. I've met Shirley many times: She's a frail, sweet, slightly foggy old woman who seems to have had a hard life. The year before the wedding, she had to stay with Angela and Mary for months while recovering from a serious illness, a period that was a financial and emotional burden for Mary, who is the breadwinner of the family. As the months wore on, Shirley witnessed the daily accumulation of caring acts that forms a family; but despite depending on this family structure in her return to health, Shirley never accepted the relationship.

Shortly after the wedding, Angela, Mary, and their girl Suzie visited Shirley in the small town where Angela grew up.

"So, do we look like a married couple?" joked Mary when they arrived.

"No," replied Shirley, her voice flat. "One of you would have to be a man."

On November 4, 2008, Californians voted to amend the state's constitution to define marriage as between "one man and one woman," thus throwing the marriages of my friends into a legal limbo. I haven't asked, but I assume that Shirley was one of the millions of Californians who voted to ban same-sex marriage. Most people of her generation, it later turned out, voted for Proposition 8; most people my age (and even more younger than me) voted against it. Most people in rural areas voted for it; most people in cities voted against.

"I was very disappointed when Prop 8 passed," Jessica's mother told me. "Jessica was depending on being able to live a legal married life with Jackie, and Prop 8 was so upsetting. But somehow I don't think it's over yet. I think it's just going to take awhile for this culture to get used to the idea."

She's right. Nationally, Prop 8 turned out to be only a setback: Within a year, Iowa, Vermont, Maine, and New Hampshire—largely rural and suburban states—all legalized same-sex marriage, joining Connecticut and Massachusetts. At this writing, Prop 8 is getting struck down or propped up every few months, as legal teams exchange blows in the courts.

But at this stage in the game, there is little doubt (at least in my mind) that marriage will ultimately open up to include people of the same sex, and that this evolutionary advance will affect every area of family law and every nook and cranny of community life. If gay men can now get married in Iowa, nothing can stop it. It's like a strapping, corn-fed freight train, roaring wholesomely past the amber waves of grain and purple mountain majesties on its way to the coastal American Sodoms. It's Iowa that is delivering same-sex marriage to San Francisco and New York, not the other way around. The old American image of the family is being carried away; a new one is coming over the horizon, but we're not there yet. The journey is changing us—all of us, Red and Blue alike—in ways that no one could anticipate.

As Exhibit A, I submit myself: Watching the battle for same-sex marriage unfold in San Francisco taught me, after a lifetime of ambivalence, that marriage might actually be worth defending. It might strike some folks as ironic that I needed a lesbian wedding to teach me that, but that's the nature of institutional renewal: Just as the black voting rights struggles of the 1960s taught previously apathetic young whites the worth of voting and civic participation, so this new civil rights struggle has something to teach us all about the value of commitment and family.

Or at least, it had something to teach me. Look, I know lots of people reading this essay think marriage is oppressive patriarchal bullshit; others might think marriage is heterosexually sacred. I'm not actually trying to convince you of anything. Instead I'm trying to describe why the struggle for same-sex marriage has been meaningful for me and for so many people in my community. The changes go much deeper than marriage: Remember how I had assumed that Jessica was the nanny? Despite being as gay-friendly as straight people come, I still had a picture in my mind of a mother and a father. That picture is gone, friends, and it's not coming back. This isn't just happening in San Francisco. It's happening all over the country.

I agree with conservatives who say that childhood is what is at stake in the same-sex marriage debates. But while they see gay and lesbian couples as the threat, to me the threat comes from bullies like Eric Roeder. My greatest fear as a father is that my son will face the same ferocious teasing and fighting I did. Worse than that, I fear that he will embrace the same solutions I did, and that he will stand back and watch other boys be teased and beaten up.

That's not the world I want him to live in; that's not the person I want him to be. From that perspective, this change that we are all going through feels like a race against time. I want the world to be entirely different by the time my son turns twelve, though I know that's impossible. I want him to be freer than I was; I want us all to be free.

Wake Up, Dads!
Tata

My child, my partner, my family are more important to me than anything else in my life. Nothing takes precedence. Nothing.

I work to support them but I am home as much as possible so we can raise our child the way we believe is the healthiest way possible. Mama does not work so she can be with our daughter 24/7. We do not place her in daycare, as we believe one or both parents should be with her, not strangers.

I pay the rent (30 percent of my income as per Housing Assistance dictum). I pay the bills. I buy the food when Food Stamps run out. I make the car payment (a fuel efficient, seven-year-old, four-cylinder Saturn wagon). I make the insurance payment. I buy the clothes from the thrift shops. Any cash at this point is coming from me. Yet, I am there to see our daughter's developmental moments. I am there to read to her, to carry her, to sing to her, to walk around the room with her as she leads me by the hand. I change her diapers and wash them. I wash clothes. I (sometimes) do dishes. I clean the bathroom. I support Mama in any way I am able when I am able. I give her kid breaks as often as possible. I comfort our daughter. I am very present in her life.

To accomplish this I work part-time. Where we live, the part-time positions do not pay a wage that can exclusively support a family. So, we are on public assistance. To stay on public assistance, one of us has to work, at least part-time. Public assistance, in this country, only provides just barely enough food if someone is working. It does not provide for your utilities. It does not allow someone not to work. It does not support families. It does not support parents. It does not support. It assists. There is a big difference.

Before moving to Menomonie, Wisconsin, I managed various businesses. I gave up that line of work because I worked forty-to-fifty-hour weeks, sometimes longer. I worked very odd hours and rarely had an uninterrupted day off—and, I almost never had two days off in a row. I worked under various degrees of stress and hazard to my health. If I was to continue that line of work, the work I am qualified to do, we would not be able to raise our daughter the way we are. If we stayed off aid under those circumstances, Mama would have to work, too, so we could afford to pay for our minimal expenses. My pay was not enough to support us all. There would be daycare required, $600 to $800 per month, so that our wee one would be watched after while Mama worked. A friend once told me, "You can get a second job to pay for daycare, be broke and not see your kid. Or, you could just be broke and be with your kid." I took his words to heart.

I guess I am a "deadbeat dad," as they say. I'm a leech. I have no pride, some may think. Am I a deadbeat because I don't work forty-to-fifty-hour weeks in a low-paying, demeaning job so my family doesn't have to suffer the indignity of being on state aid? The societal perception of those on the system says, yes. And, it is that societal perception that is a very destructive and coercive force.

In other countries the systems for supporting families vary. But, the common theme I see when I talk to or write to the folks that are from these countries is that families, and especially children and their Mamas, are supported financially. Mamas or Tatas do not have to work when parenting singly. Their health is supported with state-paid health care.

They are not punished for being poor or for choosing to raise their children in a way that benefits the child. Therefore, fathers can be home with their children more, and are supported for wanting to do so. The best quote I read was from an Australian mom on a discussion board I frequented. During one of many heated debates about public assistance, she railed on the conservative, moral majority, neocon-leaning posters and told it like it is. This country has one of the most appalling state-sponsored support systems for families in the industrialized world. The only reason people in this country not only tolerate it, but also praise and support it, is that they're used to it!

Wake up, dads! You have been had. To all the dads out there, do you really like your work so much that you would choose it over your children? Even if you are some of the few and blessed to actually love your work, is it really that hard a choice? Or, is it something else that makes the choice hard? Ask yourself, who does it benefit to maintain a system as punitive as the one that exists here in this country? What kind of society insists on ignoring the needs of a family? Of a parent? Of a child? Who does it benefit to foster a culture and an environment that says dads have to work and be away from home in order to have standing in society? Why are fathers supposed to be absent from the lives of their children? Who does this system benefit? Who indeed?

Now, I am speaking generally. There are many dads who have varying degrees of employment that would allow them to be home with their families more often. But, most dads must work to support their families in order to stay off the public assistance programs. They must do this in order to have pride. The pride that comes with being able to hold your head up and look down on those on the dole. The pride that comes with saying I have never had to ask for a handout. The pride that prevents them from being there to see their kids grow. What kind of society fosters this kind of environment? The one we all live in. That pride may one day get them the comment from their child, "I never really knew my dad. He was never around."

There is no pride in this. It is not a handout you are taking. It is the ability to put your child first. The ability to say, I want to be with my children. It is the system of punitive Puritan culture in this country that does *not* support you being at home. "The man must work to support his family." Bollocks! Raising children isn't work? It is the system that must *change*. And, with it, the attitudes of fathers toward their roles in raising their children. I want the society I live in to support my family. I want to be supported for being home with my child. I want to support other families in doing the same. I do not want to support someone else's gain over my loss. I want a just and caring society. Well, dads, we can want that till we're blue in the face. But that is definitely not what we have.

Fathers. You have been robbed of your right to be fathers. And, furthermore you have been convinced that you must participate in robbing other fathers of this right. Don't get angry at me or other dads whom your taxes support. Get angry with the entities that create the system of shame, pride, and fear that prevent you from joining us. Get angry at the system that robs you of the sight of your child's first step. Or, your child's first words. Get angry enough to change it. I paid my taxes to support this system and would happily pay more if this system actually supported families at being families, instead of being overworked and underpaid parents and children in daycare. I would rather not have my taxes support many other things that I find repulsive like war and torture. I would much prefer supporting children and their parents. But, I can't choose what happens to my money once I turn it over to the government.

For those dads who, for whatever circumstance, must work. Do what you can. Cut back your time in any way you can so you can be home more. Find the nonnecessary things in your life, the distractions, and do away with them. If you miss your children, if you wish you could be with them, isn't there any way imaginable that you could? How big a sacrifice can you make at work to make that wish come true?

Let go of pride. Let go of the stigma. Let go of fear. Don't let work be a priority. No matter what they say. No matter how much they tell you that they need you, your children need you more. Your children won't ever fire you or lay you off or force you to choose between a career and your family. They won't ever threaten you with the loss of your livelihood in order for you to comply. But, they will wish they saw you more. They will wish you were there for them. They will miss you. And, if you absolutely cannot be there, they will survive. But, take that vacation. Take that comp time—you are owed it. It's yours! Spend it with your children. If work doesn't have the coverage, that's not your problem. You have a child to raise. Make them help you raise your child if they demand your time. It's for the good of you and your family. It's for the good of your child. And, that child, your love, yourself, your family are the most important things that I can think of.

There is always another way, dads, once you want it and believe in it.

Section Five

INTERVIEWS WITH RAD DADS

It's Fucking Natural:
Ian MacKaye Talks about Parenting
Tomas Moniz

*A*fter telling my daughter I was going to interview Ian MacKaye *for* Rad Dad, *she asked, "He's the singer for the Evens, right?" And I was like, ". . . and Fugazi and Minor Threat," trying to impress her with how famous he was. She shrugged, saying, "Oh, I know Minor Threat," as if it was no big deal. She explained that the main character in her new book would go in his room and put on Minor Threat anytime he needed to be inspired. "Tell him I said hi," she said, and sauntered away. That's exactly what I did at the beginning of my conversation with Ian MacKaye about his parenting experiences.*

Tomas Moniz: Did you have any initial worries about becoming a father?

Ian MacKaye: It felt totally natural and it continues to make total sense to me. However, there are some components of being a parent that I have found troubling. The first one is a societal issue in which, for some reason, there seems to be a sort of denigration of parenthood. When you tell some people that you're gonna have a kid, they say things along the lines of, "See you in eighteen years" or "Well, you won't be sleeping anytime soon." My favorite one is, "Things are really going to change." Well, of course they're going to fucking change. That's the whole point! You don't want life to be a static experience. Change is the idea. That's why we're here.

There are two fundamental, organic things that every person experiences: birth and death. And both of these things have been draped with terror. The way so many people speak about having a child often makes it sound horrible. They always talk about the pain and the discomfort. I think the default negativity surrounding birth and children represents a deep-seated cultural mental illness.

Look at the medical world. Most doctors are trained to treat patients as people who are sick, but pregnant women are not sick. They're a different kind of patient and pregnancy is not a disease. I don't think the medical world should be using fear tactics in maternity wards, but that's the way it felt to me in our case. Our kid was born in a hospital and we had a rather negative experience with the doctor. Everything was going smooth for the nine months of the pregnancy right into labor, then the doctor arrived!

Tom: Any advice for new parents?

Ian: Trust yourself, it's natural. You just figure things out as you and the child develop; if the kid's crying, you hold him, if he's hungry, you feed him. And take the kid for a walk! Seriously. Nursing is intense, especially early on, and it's important that the mom should have some time to herself. The day that we came home from the hospital, I just took that baby and put him into a sling and took a two-hour walk and continued to do that almost every morning for the last three years. There are multiple good-nesses coming out of this practice. My partner has some time to herself in the morning and I have this really intense time that I get to spend with just him. It's a great way to get to know each other and we've done a lot of singing and had many conversations. We've also gotten to know a lot of people around the way and I've become much more connected to the neighborhood. The other day we were walking into this store and the security guard guy came up and said, "Man, I been seeing you and him walking since he was a baby." This led to a long conversation that I can't imagine ever would have occurred without the morning walks. Ultimately, I think it's very good for my son to have some one-on-one time with me, I know it's good for me to have some one-on-one time with him, and I think it's very important for my partner to have one-on-none time.

Tom: I think it's one of the things that parenting taught me: learning how to trust your own instincts about what works for you and your family and the people that you're creating your life with.

So I think that's a nice reminder that we know a lot more than we think we do.

Ian: With a child is born a parent. All of us are learning. I do think there's a danger when parents go into baby isolation and end up being the only people interacting with their child. We encouraged our friends to hold and talk to our son the second we were out in the world. It seemed important to recognize that he was a part of the world, not just *our* world. In terms of parenting, I try to avoid talking casually about kids with people. Too often it feels like talking about the weather. If somebody wants to talk about something real, something specific, maybe trying to solve a problem or mystery they've encountered with their child, I'm in, but if the extent of the conversation is going to be a report on every cute or rotten thing their child has done, I'm out. I'm not really interested in talking about kids all the time.

Tom: Well, I appreciate you doing the interview because part of my desire for doing *Rad Dad* was talking with other fathers in really profound ways. Getting beyond the pleasantries of being proud of my son or daughter or whatever it is but getting to those difficult things. When my child started getting into trouble with the court system then started doing poorly in school and reacting against the parenting that we thought we were doing a good job with, that's when your community really is important.

Ian: Your son is somebody you care about and he's fucking up. You've got to work with him, you've got to ask him, "What do we do? What the fuck do we do?" Ultimately he's going to have to weigh in on the subject. He's the one with the real answers. I think the problem is that parents often think their children's choices are somehow a reflection of them, but really it's the child's journey. For example, I think of an eight-year-old as a real person. They don't always have the best judgment because they haven't actually been able to get their mind around repercussions and consequences, but that doesn't mean they're not real. I think, quite often, children are so disenfranchised in our culture and as a result by the time they get their teenage legs on it's very easy for them to wander off, and of course they fuck up because they've never been trusted in the first place. I don't think these parents are bad, or that they did a bad job. They're just learning about it too, just learning the same damn lesson as the kid. If you operate within the moment, and you accept that everybody involved, both the parents and the kids, are real, then I think you can figure out how best to navigate any situation. It strikes me as obvious. Trust yourself and trust your kids.

Who We Be: A Q&A with Jeff Chang
Jeremy Adam Smith and Tomas Moniz

I don't remember when I met Jeff Chang. We were both activists in the Bay Area, showing up at the some of the same demonstrations and meetings, and we served on a nonprofit board together. His intelligence, integrity, and goodwill made an impression on me and on everyone he worked with—but though I knew he was a journalist who covered the hip-hop community, I didn't know anything else about his work. Then his book Can't Stop Won't Stop: A History of the Hip-Hop Generation *hit the stores, and on reading it I discovered that Jeff is a kind of journalistic superhero. He tells the social history of hip-hop, but uses it as a lens through which to view the entire history of North America since the mid-1970s. The research is astonishing; the insights are staggering. But don't take my word for it:* Can't Stop Won't Stop *won an American Book Award in 2005. Jeff's other books include* Total Chaos: The Art and Aesthetics of Hip-Hop *and the forthcoming* Who We Be: The Colorization of America. —JAS

Jeremy Adam Smith: You were a political activist for lots of years, working in antiracist, labor, and student movements. Then you became a dad. How did that affect your political activity? How do you try to integrate your kids into your political life now?

Jeff Chang: The work changed for me. I gravitated more toward board work and other sort of (I call it) tissue-building work, instead of the day-to-day type work—which also fit with my day job, such as it was. I had begun paying the bills as a full-time writer after faking it for a long while. That allowed me a lot of good daddying time. But when my book broke, and there were increased demands on my time, I was thrown out of whack. It took my very patient partner and a lot of discussions to work out a new schedule. We've been making it work now for a good few years and it's been wonderful.

Politically, I bring the kids along with me to a lot of the stuff I do. And you also tend to find and form community amongst other fathers and mothers—not to mention teachers, activists, artists, and on and on—who are doing similar work. So we've come to think of it as community-building work as well. The kids become a vital, renewing part of the equation. I began taking martial arts this year because my younger son kicks ass at it, the community around it includes so many folks doing amazing progressive work, and our *sifu* has a long history of social justice work that long pre-dates many of our friendships. It's such a beautiful thing.

Jeremy: Did becoming a dad affect your political beliefs at all? Did you find yourself looking back on stuff you said or did as an activist through the lens of fatherhood and think, that was just stupid . . . ?

Jeff: Ha! What a great question. I suppose there is a nesting instinct that occurs—and so you do find yourself going, wow, how much time did I used to spend on that? For me, also, I think that it became much less necessary to have the correct line, to work harder than the next person, in order to effect some sort of dominance in a group setting. Maybe that was just growing up too and trying to emulate my dad and some elders in my family and the community a lot more. But I did find myself able to become a devout, hard listener. It also didn't hurt that developing that skill really helped take me to the next level in my chosen field of work, writing.

Jeremy: You were also really active in hip-hop, founding the indie label SoleSides records and writing the definitive history of the hip-hop generation. What kind of father do you feel hip-hop asks you to be?

Jeff: The awesome thing about hip-hop from the beginning was the building of community. I am sad I don't get a chance to spend as much time with all of these folks I came up with, now that we've all gotten older. But I do think we share a set of values, and certainly a history, that unites us wherever we've gone.

For me, hip-hop was about bringing together a certain kind of outcast—a relentlessly questioning, somewhat avant-garde but restless for recognition, and therefore fiercely grounded kind of outcast—and SoleSides (as well as the radio work that preceded it and the writing work that continued after it) was all that for me. Hip-hop haters would never believe this but the movement introduced a criticality into all of our thinking and arts practice. It also challenged all of my radical beliefs at one point or another. But it reinforced those beliefs, surprise surprise. More than that, we always understood that this movement was ours to influence.

That's the one thing that the haters don't get: there are all kinds of hip-hops out there for those of us who claim it—just like there are all kinds of punks, all kinds of skaters, all kinds of surfers, all kinds of outcasts. All these youth movements that kicked off in the 1970s have been commercialized, it's true—but they also raised us to be *engaged*. I suppose the kind of activists (of any ideological stripe) that I dislike the most are those who assume they are the new Moses but insult the intelligence of the people they claim to uplift by refusing to do the work of engaging. I have a natural knee-jerk reaction to them, like GTFO.

Now that many of us are fathers and mothers we constantly question what we are doing in our daily practice. We must do this because we're conscious that we're responsible for our own; that's where the revolution starts. So we remain critical parents with our kids. For a long time, my kids knew I would not let them watch the BET version of it in the afternoons. At the same time, we didn't shy away from discussing the difficult issues—poverty, sexism, homophobia, all kinds of other issues—that hip-hop might raise.

I think at the end of the day, hip-hop asked us to be real. I think this is what I share with many of my peers. As much as we all want a utopian world, *this* is the world we live in. We change the world from where it's at now, not where it's supposed to be.

Tomas Moniz: My son loved reading *Can't Stop Won't Stop*—especially the history of graffiti—but as a father watching my son make choices that later lead to his trouble with the law, how can we support our children's choice and at the same time protect them from unfair consequences from the justice system?

Jeff: I don't know. One of our elders told us once that all a parent can really do is to let a child know they are unconditionally loved. The example he gave was that he knew his underage son was going to go drinking and he was forced to confront him. In the end, he chose as a father to say, "Stay safe and don't hurt anyone. If you get into a situation call me. I don't care where you are." We thought that was pretty deep. He was imagining a situation where his kid might get behind the wheel of a car or head out into the street looking for action or get arrested or worse by cops. He was saying to us, kids are always going to take risks that they shouldn't. It's part of being young. You can't be there for it all. For them to grow, sometimes it is best that you shouldn't. You can only hope that you've raised them with enough sense to know when they are heading toward a situation that may be over their head and beyond their resources. And you can only remind them that you will always be the ladder that they need.

Tom: How does the issue of race come up in your parenting?

Jeff: How does it not? Not sure where to begin . . . wanna ask it a different way?

Jeremy: Let me take a crack at answering Tom's question. I'd say race comes up in my parenting in two major ways: the fact that we're a multiracial family and the fact that my son lives in a world with people of lots of different races, some of whom have more power than others. So while we're engaged in this ongoing effort to construct our family identity, we're also part of this bigger effort to construct a multiracial world, and in age-appropriate ways I try to get that across to my son—mostly by just following his lead. When he asks me a question that touches on race, I try to answer it in a way that I think is going to contribute to that effort, to building a world where he can thrive as a multiracial person. But there's also that issue of power—we've taught him about the history of Native Americans, African Americans, the Chinese in America. He knows that there has been discrimination and violence, and I've tried to teach him to resist oppression in a hopeful way, though of course it's not always clear how to do that. All we can do as parents, I think, is to try to make our kids aware of examples, of heroes, and encourage them to be one of those heroes, not one of the villains. But also to make them aware of processes of social change—that people can take action to make things better. So that's how race comes up in my parenting.

Jeff: Thanks, Jeremy, I can really relate to that. Although we're not technically a multiracial family in the immediate sense, we both have large, very close, crazily intermarried and profoundly polycultural extended families. We look at the Obamas and we go, "That's us." Our collective roots literally span the entire globe. We contain more multitudes than Whitman ever could have imagined—or personally tolerated, for that matter—and we're proud of that.

We think it's important for our children to deeply understand the struggles our families overcame and are still going through. If they can be comfortable in their self-knowledge and sense of identity then they can be open to the world. We want our children to be able to engage people from every imaginable background with grace, openness, and humility—not ever to be suckers, but to be able to move through race, class, and identity toward possible connection, to be able to really *see* others.

So we approach our children similar to the way that you do during the teaching moments. We also reinforce the good they learn in school, correct the bad, and fill in the untaught. But we don't strain to make them politically correct. They need to know about race, class, gender, sexuality, and so much more. They need to know history and culture. We hope this knowledge will help them to understand their role in the world when they are ready to accept it. But we want them to be curious about their world, not to premake it for them. We don't want to impose a worldview they feel that they have to undo in order to arrive at their own.

In that sense we feel really blessed to have this vital, joyous, living example of what a better world can look like all around us— here in our own blood relations and in the communities into which we and all our relations all extend ourselves. When we see the kids playing with their friends and cousins, interacting across generations with their teachers, guides, uncles, aunts, and elders, it strikes us that it no longer even makes sense to call this "antiracist" practice. It's so far beyond that. It's the real meaning of being pro-life.

Jeremy: That's a beautiful way of putting it. But it strikes me that it's easy to idealize cross-generational interaction—the reality is often somewhat messy. How is your parenting different from the way you've been parented? Do you ever experience conflict with your parents or your in-laws around the ways you're raising your kids, and how do you handle it?

Jeff: I've got super parents and in-laws who support us in so many ways, allow us to do the impossible every day. I see a lot of peers who don't have that available, and it always makes me feel even more gratitude for our families. Having said that, I do think our parenting style has been strongly impacted by the way we were raised. The most important piece—perhaps even generationally—is that we were both latchkey kids. In some ways this was great. It meant we spent a lot of time at what would now be called creative play, wandering around the 'burbs, the countryside, and the beaches (for me) and the big city (for her) with friends, and becoming independent and self-sufficient early.

In some ways I see the big subcultural movements of our time—from hip-hop and punk to skateboarding and surfing and more—as being impossible without these millions of kids like us who grew up without a lot of direct parental and adult supervision. In some ways, all these activities began as simply child's play, kids filling up time and staving off boredom. That then grew into youth movements. It could be child's play with an edge, no doubt, sometimes even a predatory feel; it's no use romanticizing the whole thing. But I think the real underside of latchkey life was the abandonment that many in our generation faced, not just in desiccated family lives but in the changing state policy toward youth, from care and rehabilitation to the rending of the safety net and the casting away of kids. I think it's undeniable that American attitudes toward children have worsened considerably from the 1950s and '60s to the decades in which we grew up.

In a way, we have reacted by resolving to be very involved in our children's lives. We are acutely aware of being communicative, of balancing work with family, of *being there*, to the extent that I've sometimes recoiled at how comfortable my children are with just *hanging out at home*. I often tell them, "Get out of here! Go to the park! Hang out with your friends somewhere else!" But to no avail.

Does this make us helicopter parents with boomerang kids too? But maybe it's the memories of the latchkey life that help explain why many parents of our generation have continued the smothering parenting styles of many Boomers.

Jeremy: I think what you're saying is true, that a kind of backlash set in that resulted in very involved and even overprotective parenting. At the same time, however, I think there's other factors involved—for example, we're a much more urban culture these days, and it's harder to just cut your kids loose in the city. My family just moved, temporarily I hope, from San Francisco to suburban Palo Alto, and my son gained a lot of personal freedom with the move; he just kind of roams through our cul-de-sac in a way we could never allow on Castro St. Where do you live right now? How has parenthood changed the way you view urban life?

Jeff: We live in the wilds of South Berkeley, the part of this college town that even the supposedly progressive city leaders don't care a whit about. (If Glenn Beck only knew.) It's such a vital community, very mixed-race and class-wise and generationally. I also love that there is so much history here, made by people who consciously and courageously crossed lines—people like Angela and Fania Davis, Johnny Otis, Morrie Turner, Shirley Richardson-Brower, Don Barksdale.

But the truth is that it can get hairy out here sometimes. When shit happens, because it does, we pull together. I've often said that loving a place is like loving a person. You come to love it not only because of what it gives you, but because of what it takes away. We need each other here, unlike places where people can close the garage doors each night and never have to go next door to borrow sugar. We tend to look out for each other's kids and each other. In that sense, maybe parenthood has changed the way I view suburban life. Urban life here is a lot closer to the small country town on the windward side of O'ahu, where my mother grew up, than I ever would have imagined.

Jeremy: You mentioned a moment ago that attitudes towards kids have worsened. What changes would you like to see in how society views children? What attitudes *should* we have?

Jeff: A lot of energy these days is spent thinking about what's best for our kids, but all too often it's framed in terms of "our kids, as opposed to *their* kids." The result is a generation of middle-class aspirational parents who have created an infrastructure for kids that mirrors the dog-eat-dog meritocracy of the adult world—Kumon and soccer travel teams and beauty pageants and niche-market television channels. It's all about competition, about getting ahead, about securing comparative advantage for our kids, as opposed to *their* kids. In that sense, even childhood has become colonized by neoliberalism. It's crazy and it's crazy-making. I wonder sometimes if it's not the adults who have contracted attention deficit disorder.

If they really paid more attention to what they were doing to their children, maybe they would feel they have to medicate themselves more than they already do. In any case, corporations—pharmaceuticals, media, the culture industry—are only too happy to feed our hysteria. What happens is this: if the child is unable to perform, that is to say, "achieve," in this new crazy childhood, they get diagnosed, drugged, and shunted off to a permanent juvenilization.

Those are for the lucky ones, the ones who have the means. The larger problem is that there have been three generations now of children who have been abandoned, those who have been defined as "not our kids and not even *their* kids"—children who are poor, immigrant, of color. As a society, we've countenanced a politics of containment that enfolds them from the time they reach the age of ten. The criminalization of youth is one of the most important social issues of our era. And it is absolutely irrational. It's not even in the best interests of those who vote to support it.

Here's the math: Boomers are 75 percent white. Those under the age of eighteen will be more than 50 percent nonwhite in less than a decade. Demographer William Frey calls this "the cultural generation gap," and the states where the gap is the widest—states like Arizona, California, Texas, Florida—are where Boomers and seniors have voted to cut taxes, decimate funding for education and services for the poor, eliminate ladders to opportunity like affirmative action, and curtail immigrant rights. Who do they believe will be paying into their Social Security and Medicare accounts? What sense does it make to leave younger generations further disenfranchised and undereducated, condemned to low-wage jobs or expensive policies of containment?

The notion that *all* children are *our* children is gone; it seems so '60s, so Benjamin Spock, so Jane Addams. I don't pretend to propose any easy answers. But I am certain that if we are going to talk about creating a better society, we need to start by undoing much of what we have done to all of our children.

Daddyfreak: A Q&A with Steve Almond
Jeremy Adam Smith

*S*teve Almond wrote one of my top-ten books of the twenty-first cen-
tury, Candyfreak: A Journey Through the Chocolate Underbelly
of America. *More recently, he published another book that I like quite a
lot, the memoir* Rock and Roll Will Save Your Life. *But I truly became
a Steve Almond fan when he started writing columns about how fatherhood has changed his perspective on politics. In an op-ed for the* Boston
Globe, *for example, he attacked the disconnect between what we teach
our kids on the playground about sharing and how we run our society:*

> Can you imagine trying to justify to your child the cruel eco-
> nomic inequalities we routinely accept as part of "the American
> way"? That multimillionaires deserve tax breaks? That providing
> health insurance to our poorest citizens is some form of civic
> indulgence? That some children still go hungry in this country,
> while others live in mansions?

*Reading that, I knew I needed to talk to Steve Almond. And here's
what he had to say.*

Jeremy Adam Smith: Do you have in your mind any image of
an ideal father? Are there any dads in real life or popular culture or
literature that you see as being someone for you to emulate?

Steve Almond: Most parents have some hallowed vision of the
perfect parent—who loves unconditionally but also sets limits, who
overcomes his bullshit for the sake of the kids. But these visions are
mostly self-punishment. My own sense is that nobody knows what
the hell they're doing, especially today, with so many roles having
shifted. I know for a fact that I screw up every day, mostly out of
my own emotional neediness. I try to please the kids too much. I

lose my cool. I send mixed messages. And so on. The problem with parenting in the precincts of plenty is that fathers (and even more so mothers) hold themselves up to this impossible ideal.

As for the pastures of literature, it doesn't contain a lot of ideal dads. Nor does popular culture. The reality is that being a parent is an incredibly private, day-to-day business. It's a million little moments and decisions, not some calibrated Hollywood plot. The person I admire the most, and try to emulate, is my wife.

Jeremy: What does she do that you try to emulate?

Steve: She's just a lot more patient and thoughtful, better able to control her frustration, more organized, etc. There are exceptions, but generally speaking most dads would do really well to emulate moms. Not saying moms are perfect—nor should they be held to some higher standard. I just think they're better equipped emotionally to deal with kids, who are basically lovable but also irrational creatures.

Jeremy: What pisses you off about fatherhood, if anything? I don't mean what pisses you off about being a father—I mean about the idea of fatherhood. Or to put it a different way, do you ever feel like the kind of father you're trying to be is at odds with what kind of father the rest of society wants you to be?

Steve: Again, the main thing that pisses me off is my own weaknesses and failings. I'm not inclined to blame "society" for that. About the only large-scale thing that society wants people to be—at least in America—is consumers. But that applies to everyone.

Jeremy: Sure. So how do you raise your kids to not be little consumers without turning them into total freaks in the eyes of their peers?

Steve: Yeah, my kids are small enough that peer pressure—at least to buy stuff—isn't a factor yet. So I'm not speaking as some kind of authority. But one pretty commonsense thing would be to throw your TV out the window. It's not doing anyone any favors spiritually. We have computers and let the kids watch videos, but no commercials. We try to limit the overstimulation in general. Honestly, I'm not sure what sort of kid would consider another kid "a total freak" because they don't own enough junk. That sounds kind of crazy.

Jeremy: Hmmm. I think you're underestimating the crazy that's coming your way. I'm especially conscious of this right now because of Christmas. Now that my son's in elementary school, I see kids routinely tease or even ostracize each other based on the stuff they don't own. "What? You don't have a Wii? What a dork!" There's shame in not owning the latest crap. And actually, I think the refusal (or inability) to consume is perceived as very challenging in both the adult and kid worlds. Lots of people think my wife and I are slightly freakish for not owning a car or a TV. They seem to see it as some sort of failure—maybe I'm being paranoid and insecure, I often think some see it specifically as my failure as the father, since the father is supposed to be the breadwinner and thus the provider of junk. Our natural response has been to surround ourselves with people who also don't own cars and TVs and other crap, though of course then you start to live in a bubble. This to me is a classic parenting dilemma, for people across the political and cultural spectrum: how do you raise a child so that they can resist the negative aspects of the culture while still being equipped to thrive in that culture?

Steve: Yeah, sounds like you're facing the same dilemma we are. And you're deeper into the disconnect. I can see why you feel you're living in a bubble, but to me the slavish devotion to material crapola is the ultimate bubble. It keeps people insulated from what really matters. I'm pretty sure I'm not saying anything Christ didn't say in his Sermon on the Mount. My argument would be that, as a parent, if you're troubled by the values of the dominant culture, you should seek to change that culture, in whatever humble ways you can, and to urge your children to do the same thing. I hear you on being a breadwinner. But part of my larger point is that fathers are also moral actors, both in the small but crucial world of the family, and in the larger world.

Jeremy: I haven't made a systematic study of it or anything, but my perception is that your writing has taken a more political turn in recent years. Is that a wrong impression? If it's true, was the political turn influenced at all by becoming a dad?

Steve: Absolutely. Look, I've got skin in the game now. Back when I was single, it just didn't matter to me as much that we had a bunch of greedy, deluded maniacs holding this country's moral progress hostage. Now it does. They're fucking with my kids' future. A lot of parents—particularly prosperous, over-determined, parents like myself—get sucked inward by parenting. It's a trap, because our apathy and moral disengagement is going to cost our kids in the long run.

Jeremy: OK, so, how do you escape from that trap?

Steve: Again, I'm not an expert, just a concerned loud-mouth. My kids are quite young. But I'm guessing, based on my limited experience, that the biggest thing is the example you set. I'm not saying we read our kids the Marx-Engels Reader at night and ask that they recycle their poop, but we do try to send them the message that we're pretty lucky to have all the great stuff we have, that we shouldn't take it for granted, and that one of their big jobs is to learn to share. It will get more complicated as their awareness of the world grows. The idea is not to hide them from reality, or vice versa. But that's really a process, and an inconvenient one. Most parents are so exhausted by parenting that they tend to turn away from social responsibility, and toward convenience. That's just what Madison Avenue wants. Get the juice box. Get the SUV. Get the mollifying toy. I'm not suggesting that we do things perfectly. We don't. But we're trying in the ways we can.

Jeremy: In an op-ed you wrote for the *Boston Globe* back in 2009, you argue that all good parents are "de facto socialists," because they are constantly trying teach kids to share their stuff. What kind of response did you get to that column?

Steve: Just what you'd expect. A few people saying, "Hey, yeah, that sounds reasonable." And a ton of folks saying, "Kill that commie!" That's American discourse at the moment.

Jeremy: At the end of the piece you ask—but don't really answer—"Why are Americans afraid to express their morality in the political arena in the same way they do as parents?" Why indeed? Where does that disconnect occur?

Steve: In large part because our entire culture (and economy) is predicated on keeping all citizens in a state of insecurity and overstimulation and exhaustion. Also because the political system is fueled by special-interest money, folks who are paid, in essence, to make sure a genuine morality doesn't intrude on the business of the government. We saw a brilliant example in the extension of the Bush tax cuts. That was about greed, pure and simple, and virtually nobody would say that. The Fourth Estate, which also runs on a for-profit model, is in the business of making money, not serving as the peoples' representative in Washington. I think most Americans see "politics" as some kind of absurd sport played on cable TV. It's become unmoored from issues of morality. And, like I say, most parents simply want to get through the day however they can. Amid the inconvenience of children, they don't want the further inconvenience of having to consider themselves moral actors.

Jeremy: You write a lot about your (sometimes raunchy) life, and you've blogged for *Babble* about your first child's life as a baby. Has the relationship between your life and your writing changed because of fatherhood—for example, do you feel yourself to be reluctant to write down certain experiences? As your kids get older, how are their lives going to fit into your writing, if at all?

Steve: The more pressing question for me is how my writing is going to fit into their lives. And I don't entirely know the answer. Obviously, I've written a good deal about my life. But there is a realm of privacy, both for me and for my wife and kids, and that's something I take seriously. It's part of the reason I stopped blogging for *Babble*. And I'm sure I'll hold back on writing more and more stuff as they and their friends become readers. Nobody wants to go through adolescence with their dad taking notes and writing "humorous" columns about them. That being said, my wife and I hope we're raising the sort of kids who recognize the value of storytelling. (We had considered not teaching the children to read, but they seem to be picking it up pretty quickly.) My hunch is that they'll want nothing to do with our work. But we certainly can't hide what we do. Honesty is always the best policy. Or at least, the inevitable one.

The Beautiful Struggle:
A Q&A with Ta-Nehisi Coates
Jeremy Adam Smith

W hen I interviewed Ta-Nehisi Coates back in 2008 for my book
The Daddy Shift, he had just been laid off as a reporter for
Time *magazine and had returned to his old job as a stay-at-home dad,
and his days in Harlem consisted of taking his son to the doctor, picking
him up from football practice, doing laundry, making dinner for his family. Then six months after we talked his memoir* The Beautiful Struggle
appeared and he started blogging for the Atlantic *magazine, and suddenly Ta-Nehisi Coates was famous and acclaimed—in one representative blurb, the writer Walter Mosley hails Coates as "the young James
Joyce of the hip-hop generation." Here's a partial, edited transcript of
our original conversation.*

Jeremy Adam Smith: How old were you when you became a
father?

Ta-Nehisi Coates: I was twenty-four when Samori was born.
And you know, that didn't strike me as young. I didn't understand.
I didn't grow up in poverty or anything like that, but I grew up in
west Baltimore in the '80s and what I knew of the world, people
had kids at that age. That's what I knew. Once I got to the professional world it became clear to me that at certain class levels people
don't do that. I mean, they have kids at thirty-eight or whatever,
when they're stable and everything.

But that didn't dawn on me at twenty-four. I was very eager to be a father. I defined fatherhood as part of manhood. It's
funny—today I talk to a lot of my friends who grew up a little differently and they have a strong sense of themselves as individuals
and I don't think I had that. I think I was very much about the idea

that there was some sort of responsibility to African Americans to have children, to father children, to be an involved father, to be a good father—you know, to produce soldiers. That's how I thought about it. I guess to some extent I still think about it that way.

Jeremy: Tell me more about that—when you were growing up, what images did you see of fathers and fatherhood?

Ta-Nehisi: I came up at a time when there was all this talk—real or invented, didn't matter—but the mythology was black men are not being fathers. Black men are not kicking in. They're not fully doing their part.

But that wasn't true in my family. My mom, for most of the relationship, she made more money than my dad but my dad was taking care of us every day. I don't think they'd characterize themselves as feminist, but there was this sort of applied feminism going on. Betty Friedan's problems are not particularly familiar to African American people—you know, the whole thing of the women staying at home the guy going to work and providing the income. That's not familiar to large swaths of poor and working-class women either, but certainly not in our communities. I'm sure there were some families like that, with dad at work and mom at home. But my grandparents certainly weren't like that. My parents weren't like that.

There probably were gendered roles in my house. I'm sure there were and I'm sure my mother would tell you that there were. I'm speaking from a child's perspective, though. That wasn't how I saw it.

Jeremy: Even so, you seem to be implying that your family was unusual, in that your father was so involved.

Ta-Nehisi: None of my friends had fathers. I was definitely in the minority. In my neighborhood, you fell into one of three camps: there was the minority like me who lived with their father; there were people who did not live with their father but knew who their father was; then a great majority of people either did not know who their fathers were or had not had contact with them in many years.

Jeremy: Earlier, you referred to "the mythology of black men not being fathers." But you're saying it was more than just a myth.

Ta-Nehisi: It was something to fight against. At that time, I processed it as a sort of fall from glory—that we had not always been like that. I'm not sure if that's true, but that's the way I processed it, as a fall from glory. And I very much wanted to be a part of, you know, reversing that fall—I thought fatherhood was the ultimate service to black people. It was almost a nationalist, Afrocentric way of seeing it. I felt I was the product of a great, great father and that I had a responsibility to go forward and try to live that out as best I could.

Jeremy: You were a stay-at-home dad when your son was a baby and you're a stay-at-home dad now—you just got laid off. Does it trouble you, not making money?

Ta-Nehisi: My partner has always made more money than me, except for maybe one or two years we've been together. This is our tenth year now. You know, getting laid off is always a difficult thing, but it gave me back time with my son. I mean, that's just absolutely huge. I take him to school and then pick him up at the bus stop after school. He played little league football this summer, so I would take him to practice. I make doctor's appointments and make sure he does his homework. I cook lots of meals; I'm kind of a foodie. And to me, it's just natural. And I guess that's because of my parents.

I guess not making much money would trouble me, if I felt like I wasn't a very good father. If I didn't have anything else to bring to the relationship, then, yes, it would trouble me. If you are a man who thinks that what you bring to a relationship is economic power and that's it, then I guess that would trouble you. What else is your claim to the relationship? I'm just glad I wasn't raised that way.

Revolutionary Dignity and Daughters:
A Q&A with Jeff Conant
Tomas Moniz

Tomas Moniz: Can you tell us about some of the projects you have been a part of over the last few years?

Jeff Conant: Aside from raising a daughter and trying to earn a living, you mean? I recently published my book *A Poetics of Resistance*, about the Zapatista movement. Much of that was actually researched and written over a decade ago, though, when I lived in Chiapas. I also published in 2008 a book that took eight years to complete, called *A Community Guide to Environmental Health*, a grassroots educational manual on everything from compost toilets to toxic waste. That book involved travel to communities around the world struggling to address environmental degradation and the livelihood costs associated with it. It's from the base of that work that I now find myself doing media work with a number of climate justice organizations, essentially trying to get the word out about solutions to the ecological crisis that are both just and ecological, as opposed to market-driven. I'm also developing popular education materials on human rights issues, and doing some freelance journalism, and trying to make time for some fiction and creative nonfiction projects I've had going for too many years now. And playing with puzzles and Play-Doh and going to the zoo.

Tom: Was it a specific choice to become a parent?

Jeff: It was, but not an easy one. I had always been ambivalent about children—both having them and being around them—undoubtedly because my own family was pretty troubled: alcoholic, estranged parents, a mother who was severely depressed and eventually died of alcohol-induced dementia, a sister who to this day does not communicate with me, all of which, my experience told me, was part of the package of the nuclear family. That is, the whole idea of family has always given me trouble, because for me family was the source of my greatest pain. So when I found myself partnered up with a woman who was bound and determined to have a child and was a midwife besides, I decided, not without real psychic challenges, to let things go in that direction. Actually, I said let's have five years together, and if we make it we'll have a kid. Five years later, we decided to go for it. And now, of course, I fall in love with every kid I see, and I see this as the greatest gift I've ever received.

Tom: How do you see parenting as a political act?

Jeff: I see every act as political, and parenting more than most. If politics is about the use and management of social power, then what could be more political than the decision to take responsibility for another human being? The decision to intentionally help shape another's life and have one's own life shaped in return, the commitment to engage in community at the level necessary for child-rearing, to engage in education, the commitment to self-consciously help direct another person's experience of the world, and to share the most profound aspects of humanity. And, if radical politics is about challenging concentrations of power and promoting ethical action, which I believe it is, then parenting is about imparting ethical beliefs, and engaging on a daily basis with the praxis of transforming "power-over"—coercive power—into "power-with"—shared, social power. By the way, my daughter's, uh, three, so "praxis" might be a big word here.

Tom: I am very interested in hearing about your attempt to integrate your role as a parent and an activist (both successfully and at times unsuccessfully); or, how has parenting informed your activism.

Jeff: Given that Sacha is barely three, I wouldn't say there's tremendous integration, except to the extent that I am an activist living and working in a community of activists, so there is a shared commitment among those we parent with, to do things in a way that is consistent with our beliefs. Sacha's mom is a midwife, which is a tremendous form of community service, personal, spiritual service, and activism, so doing my best to support that, is part of it too. And, for better or worse, my work, my activism, involves international travel—basically I advocate and document struggles for environmental human rights at an international level—so just balancing my travel, my partner's midwifery, and raising a child as attentively as possible—it ain't easy, but it's all part of the commitment to making the world a better place. And yes, failure to get it right is definitely a part of it—which, honestly, can be refreshing in a world where we're so programmed against failure of any sort. But that's where the growth happens, isn't it?

So, how has parenting informed my activism? It's cliché (what about parenting isn't cliché?) but it's true that it gives my work deeper meaning. Soon after Sacha was born I remember thinking, I spent most of my youth and young adulthood feeling angry—politically angry, personally angry—and I finally worked past a lot of that anger while still engaging in the work of fighting injustice, and now, I'm going to be angry all over again. Because when you see failing schools, laws targeting youth, toxic chemicals everywhere, in everything, and the tremendous insensitivity of this country and this world to the most basic of human needs, and when you're seeing that in the light of your own child's needs, it is extremely difficult— for me, anyway—to not get mad and then to want to take action. And . . . especially internationally, I find that people take me and my work more seriously because I'm a parent. As my partner said to me during the difficult transition into parenthood, "Welcome to the human race." I think when people know you are handling something beyond your own more-or-less-selfish interests, something that everyone knows is extremely difficult and yet driven by fierce personal commitment, it automatically generates respect, which builds connection, which is, simply put, good for organizing.

And of course, let's not forget the love. The love you feel for your child is so profound, so transformative, so encompassing, that it touches everything you do. If your work is to influence the workings of the world, then a superabundance of love is bound to have some positive impact on that work, and ideally that love gets spread to some degree through the work.

Tom: What is your most humbling moment as a parent?

Jeff: That is a terrible question, because all those moments rush to compete with each other in the front of my brain. There are a lot of proud moments—beginning with having caught my daughter when she was born. But humbling, or worse, humiliating moments, there are many. They almost always have to do with me wanting to do something other than attend immediately to the child's needs, and maybe being in a frustrating moment with my partner, and getting angry beyond reason. There were a few times, at least a few, where the baby was screaming and I was screaming too because actually managing the situation was beyond me. At one of those moments, this was perhaps the very worst, I was alone with my daughter and she was maybe six months old, and she wouldn't stop hollering, and I threw something, a spoon I think, across the kitchen and it hit a drinking glass and the glass shattered, and suddenly I have a screaming baby and broken glass everywhere, and I am *damn* lucky there was no injury. And, you know, after a moment like that everything seems to get real quiet, and you take a deep breath, and you clean up the glass and soothe the baby and by the time you're done you're in a different mood altogether. So, yeah, every truly humbling moment seems to be about my needs being in competition with the child's needs—and when you are suddenly forced to realize that you're competing with a one-year-old, that I think is the very definition of humbling.

Tom: In what ways do you see fathers as nurturers?

Jeff: Fatherhood is an opportunity to nurture, and I think men need these opportunities. Not to impress, not to give because you're going to get something back, but to simply, deeply, sweetly, care for that child. It is a very healing role to play, and a wonderful way to spend time on this earth. And of course there are many ways to nurture—play can be nurture, teaching, reading aloud, or just holding the child. Sometimes I think one of the most nurturing things is not to do what we think of as nurturing, you know, soothing and saying, "It's OK, Dada's here," but to say, "What's it like for you? What are you experiencing right now?" Which is, of course, not what men in general are raised to do.

Tom: I really enjoyed your book about how the Zapatistas use storytelling and mythology to create their identity, to in fact make their dreams a reality. In what ways has studying the Zapatistas and working with them taught you about family or about parenting or raising children?

Jeff: One of the most essential things I learned in the few years I worked in Zapatista communities is summed up in something a Zapatista friend said to me once: "Our struggle is not for us, but for our grandchildren." Despite the urgency to address injustice and oppression right now, being indigenous, the Zapatistas take the long view, and they taught me that, not only do things rarely change overnight, the greatest results of our work are not necessarily even seen in our lifetimes. Could anything be more true of parenthood than that?

Secondly, the mythology, all the language the Zapatistas use to bring their ideologies to life can, in some ways, be invoked by one word that they use a lot: dignity. Dignity, for the Zapatistas, means the right and the ability to live to one's full potential. If anything radical is at the heart of my own parenting, it is a desire to raise my daughter with that sense of revolutionary dignity—that she should have that, and she should impart it to others.

Movements and Storytelling:
A Q&A with Raj Patel
Tomas Moniz

*R*aj Patel inspires me. In his essays and his books—his most recent is The Value of Nothing—*he writes in a clear, engaging, informal way that immediately draws me in. And yet he weaves in such support and evidence and details that his points—about food politics and food justice, about value and commodity, about living an engaged, authentic life—just seem so amazingly obvious, so natural. He makes the struggle seem so worth it, so destined for victory. The remarkable thing about Raj, an economist by training, is that he has both worked for the World Bank and the World Trade Organization—and protested against these institutions. As a result, he brings an insider's knowledge to a radical critique of capitalism and consumption.*

I was ecstatic that he agreed to talk with me about parenting, about connecting the global world with the world in our living rooms, about the inspiration found and the need for storytelling.

Tomas Moniz: So where shall we begin?

Raj: I'd like to talk about this profeminist men's movement in Zimbabwe I used to work with, not just because I've got a kid, but also because I'm interested in gender, masculinity, capitalism. If we're serious as radical fathers about understanding capitalism and understanding the root of where it is we find ourselves today as parents, then it's certainly worth understanding the social systems in which we live and the kinds of divisions of labor that come with capitalism.

So, I was lucky enough to work in Zimbabwe with a group called Padare. The word is a useful kind of subversion because 'padare' is the Shona word for the men-only space where patriarchs get together to make decisions for everyone. This group called themselves Padare: The Men's Forum on Gender, where they were doing a lot of work around domestic violence, sort of taking on the challenge of how to stop domestic violence as men. How do men stop other men from being involved in domestic violence? These are men, social workers and teachers and actors and others, who were taking seriously the idea that we just can't sit back and let women do the campaigning. We are responsible and there are things we can do. And in fact, we ought not to feel disempowered by this. We can do street theater, media work, going into schools and talking with boys in particular, but talking to everyone about gender and about domestic violence and how to stop that.

They're also moving into thinking not just about domestic violence, but the sort of social situation that domestic violence happens in; they were taking seriously the idea that capitalism does a lot to shape the conditions of domestic violence. They were doing some amazing activism around education and thinking about men's roles in the home, about labor in the home: who does the cooking, who does the cleaning. When last I saw them in 2002, they were actively recruiting. They recruited men in what could sometimes be a very patriarchal society into thinking in new ways about representation, about gender, about how men might be living their lives differently, and it was mind-blowing.

Tom: This doesn't fit with most people's images of Africa.

Raj: It's important particularly in light of how many people in the west stereotypically think of Africa. People think, "Oh, Africa, that's the place where people go to die, where children are born with flies in their eyes," and—other than the end of apartheid—we might learn nothing radical about gender or about movements for liberation in Africa.

And yet here were men who were actually making it happen in a way that frankly I haven't seen in the United States, at least not in this kind of committed way. We don't need to put them on a pedestal. I mean, like you and me, they were imperfect. They were no less prone to the kind of casual sexism that we all are and that we've been brought up in and we strive to fight against. There's no point in romanticizing anything. But what is worth celebrating is the fact that they were people who were willing to take it on, to see what they could do to be better, and I love that.

Tom: That's a really powerful story. And I've said many times storytelling is so important in parenting. The stories we tell ourselves and our children, stories of people stepping up to do these kinds of things. I was thinking when you were telling me this, how has knowing this kind of history, knowing about these organizations, come to impact the way you're thinking about parenting your own child?

Raj: Whether it's TV or whether it's the media, there's just a whole shitload of things out there that feels beyond our control. And so, this overwhelming feeling sets up an individualistic mode of radical parenting, which believes that, "I'm going to shield my kids from television" and "We're going to go nowhere near a McDonald's." And of course that's important, but it is a very neoliberal attitude in that sense of thinking that, "It's just me and my family unit against The Man all by ourselves." That's very individualistic.

We need movements.

That's why I'm excited to be part of the food justice movement where we're saying what we want to do is stop the capitalist advertising of food to kids; that's a campaign. It's not just an individual action—though of course individual action matters—but getting involved in campaigns means building a community of parents who also don't want their kids poisoned by the fast-food industry or poisoned by certain sexist or racist representations.

Tom: Consumerism and advertizing I feel are like my biggest archenemies. Because they suck me in as well—I'm a sucker for the latest movie trailer. But I'm an adult, I like to think. My thirteen-year-old daughter is not. She is incredibly articulate and empathetic, but she is obsessed with shopping. You know, Target, Old Navy, H&M. How can we begin to combat some of the consumer pressure that these twelve, thirteen, fourteen-year-old children are under?

Raj: Any advertizing to kids under the age of eight is unconscionable because kids are unable to tell the difference between advertising and lies. That's not to say that the children cannot tell that they're being advertised to. They know that they're being advertised to. But they can't evaluate the truth. By advertising to them while they're so young, corporations are essentially handicapping their ability to choose for themselves.

Globally, for every dollar that is spent advertising food that is good for you, $500 is spent advertising crap that will harm our children. In a sense, and here's a contradiction, that's what we're doing by campaigning against corporate advertising against children—you are creating better consumers because they are more likely to be able to make rational decisions. Capitalism depends on people making irrational decisions and not rational decisions, right? Because otherwise your daughter wouldn't be interested in the kinds of things that she's interested in. There's little that's rational about the unrealistic body types, the unattainable lifestyle, et cetera. But the whole point of advertising is to make you postpone thinking about that sort of stuff rationally or critically. And instead just head straight for your desires rather than for your capacity for rational thinking. That's why I think campaigning against food advertising becomes a very useful tool.

And there has been success: removing toys from happy meals in San Francisco is perhaps the most high profile. There's a huge reaction to that victory, particularly from the food industry, because they can see where this ends and where this ends is that actually we do end up being smarter consumers, eating more healthily—and better able to evaluate the shit that we are fed by capitalism. And, if we're more able to defend ourselves against its seductions, it means we're better able to imagine and build something better than capitalism.

Tom: I'm wondering now that you've become a parent how your relationship to your partner and to your activism has changed.

Raj: Feminist economists taught me that labor, including reproductive labor, should be rewarded, reduced, and redistributed—those are the three R's of reproductive labor. The idea that actually reproductive labor, whether that's childrearing or cooking or building a community, which generally goes unpaid and generally is done by women, needs to be paid first. It needs to be rewarded.

Then it needs to be recognized, of course.

And then it needs to be redistributed so that there is more gender equity in that work. I try and walk the talk, but it's hard sometimes to live an antisexist life when you have been brought up in a world that is so incredibly sexist. That's not my struggle alone; it's every man's struggle.

And as for my activism, frankly, ever since having a kid, I moved from having a very sort of deep, intellectual conviction to something I feel in the marrow of my bones. I remember back in the day when we were doing stuff around the World Trade Organization. It was important to have a daycare facility, to have daycare arranged and to have things at a time of day where people could actually join in. But it felt like an encumbrance. It felt like, "Oh god, I forgot about that," whereas now it's like obviously you have to do that. And I do it much more joyfully now than I did in the past.

Tom: Was it a conscious choice to become a parent? Did you have fears initially? And how did they manifest, or not manifest once you became one?

Raj: Oh, absolutely. I mean, when looking at the state of the world today, climate change and the global food system and understanding how much trouble we're in right now, it's not an easy decision to want to become a father. But yes, I did want to become a father. Initially, we were hoping that we would have a girl and then we had a boy.

I was really scared about how to bring up a boy in this world without fucking him up as I have been. I want to equip him with tools he needs to shield himself, to fight back against the kinds of injustices and inequalities that, to some extent are getting much, much worse now than they were even when I was growing up. I worry about getting my son ready or artful in the ways of resistance without militarizing him in that way. I mean, I know that it's possible to resist without succumbing to these tropes of masculinity. It's possible to resist with love and compassion and with beauty and with a great deal of smarts and guile and humor and courage.

That's why I enjoy reading *Rad Dad*, because, you know, I'm already sort of aware of things that I ought and ought not to be doing. But in a sense, no one can make these mistakes but me and my kid. And I hope that when I do make these mistakes that I don't fuck him up too badly. But we can learn from others. This brings us back to storytelling because inspiration can happen pretty much anywhere, in the pages of *Rad Dad*, in our communities and campaigns, even in Africa and in homes and communities across the world.

CONCLUSION

Storytelling
Tomas Moniz

Parenting starts with a story:

My grandma, worried that her three-year-old son had not spoken a word yet, had him chase down a grasshopper. Diligently, without complaint, the boy did, and returned with a smile. *Open*, she said. Confused, with hesitation, he opened wide. Wide. She shoved the grasshopper in and closed his mouth. *Hablas, mijo, hablas.* He spit it out, crying. Crying and yelling. *He has not stopped either since*, she says, and smiles, thinking of her now-fifty-year-old son talking his time away in a New Mexican state penitentiary.

That son is my father. He smiles when he tells this story to my children on a snowy day in his trailer on the outskirts of town. He has been out of jail for a year now. My kids look to me for guidance: *Do we believe?* I can only smile. Teasing, my father says, *What, mija, you don't believe me? Come here I'll tell you more.*

I realize this is so central to my parenting. Stories. But I did not know this when I became a father. I didn't know those afternoons or early mornings when my partner had to leave to culinary school and I had to discover what to do for the next eight hours that I was talking to both my newborn son and myself. I was showing us the way. I was imagining the path home. Telling myself, telling my son that success was possible, that despite my fear, my ignorance, my loneliness, this path was traversable. It's the stories that we tell each other that create connections, that foster empathy, that teach.

But we aren't the only ones telling tales. I see now how storytelling works at a cultural, social level as well; how myths of capitalism, Christianity, patriarchy are told over and over and over until our kids tell them back to each other while at play, to their teachers in their homework, to us if we listen during those tucking-in times or in the quiet hours when we wake up together in our bed. This is linguistic terrorism. I have also come to see how our cultural stories that impact our kids more than any one thing can, more than parents, more than teachers.

My daughter, combing her hair in the morning, sulks away from the mirror, saying her hair is ugly. Who taught her that beauty standard? Because no amount of *oh no it doesn't, honey* is going to change her mind in that moment. My other daughter informing her sister as they play in the car that if she ever lives with a boy then she has to have sex with him. *Really, why?* my partner asks. *Because*—as if that explains it. We need stories to counter these. We need heroes, legends, rituals that offer other narratives, other examples of how to look, how to live, what should be valued, what holds meaning, what it means to be alive.

Because that shit works. My son was a vegetarian for five years (on his own accord) but now laughs at that *Super Size Me* film—not because of what it's saying but because it took the guy twenty whole minutes to eat his meal, and then he puked. *Hella stoopid. I'd eat two in ten minutes*, my son brags. As if it's something to be proud of. My son—whose biggest dream right now is to own a scraper to cruise through south Berkeley bumping bass because it looks tight. Yes, that's my son, but so is this: My son taking his three-year-old cousin by the hand to walk in the back yard. The cousin picks up a worm. He asks her has she ever heard the story about Ella who ate a big ol' worm when she was a baby, thinking it was a Cheeto? *Ever since then*, he says, *Ella is a little animal lover. I think it's the worm inside her.* They laugh and laugh. I can only smile. I don't know what it means, what the moral is, but I know my son is gonna make it. In his own way, on his own terms. But he's gonna survive all the lies that are forced on him and so many others like him. All the bullshit he's asked to believe or buy into.

What are the stories you need to tell? What do you share with your child, your lovers, your family and friends?

Our strongest weapons are our stories, the stories we tell our children, the ones we whisper to each other in beds of our own making, the myths that fill our imaginations, shared among conspirators at bars or over camp fires or sitting in jail cells. It is those weapons we must employ over and over to create the world we want. I have realized that of all the things that give my life meaning it has been the spoken visions of the future or the shared memories of the past that sustain me in the present, that nurture my growth, my will, my determination. In stories, facts become fictitious, desire and purpose mold the outcome. If I need to hear stories of survival, if I need to find inspiration, if I need to laugh and laugh and laugh, I need only open my mouth, need only to sit with someone close and say, *Tell me a story*. Here is one of my favorites to tell my kids when they ask why I do what I do. And I swear it is all true.

At twenty, a few months before the birth of my son, I hitch-hiked from Las Vegas, through New Mexico, down the highway to the state penitentiary just outside of Santa Fe to see my father face to face. To try to find some answers, to perhaps find guidance. He tells me he fucked up. He should be out there with me, working with me, living life with me. *Because*, he says, *I realized I'm a slave in here. And now I can only fight against other slaves. But if I was out there with you, when I realized I was a slave, I coulda done something, I coulda fought back at least. Somehow. In here, it's just fucked up. All you can do is write and fight.*

My father explained that in jail, pencils are like daggers, you can write and you can stab. *Mira*, he points to his hand, *here are the pencil tips that I cannot get out.*

Welcome to radical fatherhood.

Contributor Biographies

Steve Almond is the author of *Candyfreak* and *Rock and Roll Will Save Your Life*, as well as the story collections *My Life in Heavy Metal* and *The Evil B.B. Chow*.

Jack Amoureux is an assistant professor at American University and a fan of Boise State University football. He lives in Washington, D.C., with his wife, Angela, and their child, Ocean.

Mark Andersen is a punk rock activist and author who lives in the Columbia Heights neighborhood of Washington, DC. He cofounded the punk activist collective Positive Force DC in 1985, and is now codirector of We Are Family, an outreach and advocacy organization that works with seniors in inner-city DC. He is the author of two books, *Dance of Days: Two Decades of Punk in the Nation's Capitol* and *All the Power: Revolution Without Illusion*.

Mike Araujo is the father of Xavier George Brown Araujo and the son of George and Frances Araujo. He is a grip and a rigger, he loves his union, and he is working for the social revolution.

Jeff Chang is the author of *Total Chaos: The Art and Aesthetics of Hip-Hop* and *Can't Stop Won't Stop: A History of the Hip-Hop Generation*, which won an American Book Award in 2005. His writings have appeared in publications such as *URB*, *Bomb*, *San Francisco Chronicle*, the *Village Voice*, the *San Francisco Bay Guardian*, *Vibe*, *Spin*, the *Nation*, and *Mother Jones*.

Ta-Nehisi Coates is a contributing editor to the *Atlantic* magazine and author of *The Beautiful Struggle*.

Jeff Conant is a writer, educator, and social-justice activist with a focus on international development and ecology. His book, *A Poetics of Resistance: the Revolutionary Public Relations of the*

Zapatista Insurgency (AK Press, 2010) examines the cultural politics of the Zapatista movement of Chiapas, Mexico, focusing on the Zapatistas' persuasive use of symbolic language and colorful imagery to bring their struggle to the world's attention.

Cory Doctorow is a science fiction author, activist, journalist, and blogger. He is the coeditor of Boing Boing and the author of *The Great Big Beautiful Tomorrow* and Tor Teens/HarperCollins UK novels such as *For the Win* and the bestselling *Little Brother*. Born in Toronto, Canada, he now lives in London.

Jason Denzin is a father and tech activist interested in seeing our world go from war- and profit-based to peace- and people-based.

Craig M. Elliott II practices love and compassion living with his partner, Nicole, their two children, Jackson and Thomas, and a host of family animals in Northern California. He is a revolutionary-at-heart, a dancer-in-spirit, and a lover of true beings. Craig appreciates good coffee, laughing fully, and cooking with his kids. Craig can be contacted at celliott@samuelmerritt.edu.

Chip Gagnon is a former stay-at-home dad who lives in Ithaca, New York, with his wife Lisa and kids Nell (20) and Lucas (17). He misses the times when a big hug was enough to solve all of his kids' worries but has enjoyed experiencing their growth into the wonderful people they've become.

Keith Hennessy is a San Francisco–based performance artist, teacher, choreographer, and organizer who tours internationally.

David L. Hoyt, known to the blog-o-sphere as Chicago Pop, lives in Chicago's Hyde Park neighborhood. He is trained as a scholar of European history and now writes and blogs on a range of topics while keeping an eye on his very curious son and his shortly arriving daughter.

Simon Knaphus is a birth-giving transgender papa and radical lawyer. He lives in the Bay Area but dreams of a more rural existence.

Ian MacKaye cofounded Dischord Records as a teenager in 1980 and went on to form the bands Minor Threat, Fugazi, and the Evens.

Tomas Moniz is the founder, editor, and a writer for the award-winning zine *Rad Dad*. He has helped raise three children and has been making zines since the late 1990s. He also is a teacher at Berkeley City College, teaching basic skills classes, and works with the National Writing Project. You can check out more about his personal and professional projects at www.tomasmoniz.com.

Zappa Montag is a father, educator, concerned citizen, music addict, and a few other things. He was born in New York, lived in the Bay Area as a small child, and spent his formative years in Mendocino County. He sees life as art in progress and tries to take a little creative license in all of his endeavors.

Raj Patel is an award-winning writer, activist, and academic. His first book was *Stuffed and Starved: The Hidden Battle for the World Food System* and his latest, *The Value of Nothing*, is a *New York Times* best-seller.

Jeremy Adam Smith is the founder of the acclaimed blog *Daddy Dialectic*, author of *The Daddy Shift*, coeditor of *Are We Born Racist?*, and a 2010–11 John S. Knight Journalism Fellow at Stanford University. His essays, short stories, and articles have appeared in the *Nation*, BusinessWeek.com, *Mothering*, *San Francisco Bay Guardian*, *San Francisco Chronicle*, *Utne Reader*, *Wired*, and numerous other periodicals and books. Jeremy has also been interviewed by many media outlets, including *The Today Show, The Talk*, the *New York Times*, *USA Today*, Salon.com, *Nightline*, and numerous NPR shows.

Jason Sperber is the stay-at-home dad of two daughters, ages seven and two, and husband of a family physician. A former high school social studies teacher and online journalism community manager, he writes from Bakersfield, California. Read his blogs, *Daddy in a Strange Land* and *Rice Daddies*, and follow his tweets at @dad_strangeland.

Burke Stansbury is a social justice activist and organizer in Washington, D.C. He writes regularly about parenting and disabilities on his son's blog, http://lucascamilo.com.

Tata is an anonymous parent who lives somewhere on the planet Earth.

Shawn Taylor is a father, a partner, and a writer, in that order. He is the author of *Big Black Penis: Misadventures in Race and Masculinity* and *People's Instinctive Travels and the Paths of Rhythm* for the 33 1/3 series, and the e-book *LovePunk Manifesto*.

Jeff West is a full-time father of two in Lexington, Kentucky. He blogs about contemporary parenting at http://www.postindustrialparenthood.blogspot.com/.

Mark Whiteley is a thirty-four-year-old Bay Area native, husband and father to the three most beautiful ladies in the world, internationally published and exhibited author and photographer, skateboarder for twenty-seven years, former editor-in-chief of a large skateboard magazine/website and current social media manager for Nike, Inc. He has been a featured speaker at the San Francisco Exploratorium and the University of California at Santa Cruz, has slept under the stars in New Zealand and in a metal shed in Alaska, enjoys John Fahey, Cormac McCarthy, movies, sweater weather, sarcasm, self-deprecating humor, the Japanese concept of "mono no aware," and also run-on sentences.

My Baby Rides the Short Bus:
The Unabashedly Human Experience of
Raising Kids with Disabilities
Edited by Yantra Bertelli, Jennifer Silverman,
Sarah Talbot

978-1-60486-109-9
336 pages
$20

In lives where there is a new diagnosis or drama every day, the stories in this collection provide parents of "special needs" kids with a welcome chuckle, a rock to stand on, and a moment of reality held far enough from the heart to see clearly. Featuring works by "alternative" parents who have attempted to move away from mainstream thought—or remove its influence altogether—this anthology, taken as a whole, carefully considers the implications of parenting while raising children with disabilities.

From professional writers to novice storytellers including Robert Rummel-Hudson, Ayun Halliday, and Kerry Cohen, this assortment of authentic, shared experiences from parents at the fringe of the fringes is a partial antidote to the stories that misrepresent, ridicule, and objectify disabled kids and their parents.

Reviews:
"This is a collection of beautifully written stories, incredibly open and well articulated, complicated and diverse: about human rights and human emotions. About love, and difficulties; informative and supportive. Wise, non-conformist, and absolutely punk rock!" —China Martens, author of *The Future Generation: The Zine-Book for Subculture Parents, Kids, Friends and Others*

"If only that lady in the grocery store and all of those other so-called parenting experts would read this book! These true-life tales by mothers and fathers raising kids with "special needs" on the outer fringes of mainstream America are by turns empowering, heartbreaking, inspiring, maddening, and even humorous. Readers will be moved by the bold honesty of these voices, and by the fierce love and determination that rings throughout. This book is a vital addition to the public discourse on disability." —Suzanne Kamata, editor of *Love You to Pieces: Creative Writers on Raising a Child with Special Needs*

"This is the most important book I've read in years. Whether you are subject or ally, *My Baby Rides the Short Bus* will open you—with its truth, humanity, and poetry. Lucky you to have found it. Now stick it in your heart." —Ariel Gore

As a not-for-profit*, collectively-run publisher and distributor of zines and related work, Microcosm Publishing strives to add credibility to zine writers and their ethics, teach self empowerment, show hidden history, and nurture people's creative side! Based in Leavenworth, KS and Portland, OR, Joe Biel started the distro and then-record-label out of his bedroom in 1996. Since then it's grown to become one of the largest zine distributors in the world, reaching an international audience through our website and retail store.

* (We operate central to a mission statement and are financially not for profit, but we are not a 501c3 organization because it does not allow us to self-manage.)

....

BE OUR BFF FOR 6 MONTHS!

Do you love what Microcosm publishes? Do you want us to publish more great stuff? Would you like to receive each new title as it's published? If your answer is "yes!", then you should subscribe to our BFF program. BFF subscribers help us pay for printing new books, zines, DVDs, and more. They also ensure that we can continue to print great material each month! Every time we publish something new we'll send it to your door!

Subscriptions are based on a sliding scale of $10-30 per month. Please give what you can afford so that we can be sure to send out more stuff each month. Include your t-shirt size and month/date of birthday for a possible surprise!

Minimum subscription period is 6 months.

Microcosm Publishing
636 SE 11th Ave
Portland, OR 97214-2405
www.microcosmpublishing.com

PM Press was founded at the end of 2007 by a small collection of folks with decades of publishing, media, and organizing experience. PM Press co-conspirators have published and distributed hundreds of books, pamphlets, CDs, and DVDs. Members of PM have founded enduring book fairs, spearheaded victorious tenant organizing campaigns, and worked closely with bookstores, academic conferences, and even rock bands to deliver political and challenging ideas to all walks of life. We're old enough to know what we're doing and young enough to know what's at stake.

We seek to create radical and stimulating fiction and non-fiction books, pamphlets, t-shirts, visual and audio materials to entertain, educate and inspire you. We aim to distribute these through every available channel with every available technology—whether that means you are seeing anarchist classics at our bookfair stalls; reading our latest vegan cookbook at the café; downloading geeky fiction e-books; or digging new music and timely videos from our website.

PM Press is always on the lookout for talented and skilled volunteers, artists, activists and writers to work with. If you have a great idea for a project or can contribute in some way, please get in touch.

PM Press
PO Box 23912
Oakland CA 94623
510-658-3906
www.pmpress.org